puppy handbook

HOW TO CHOOSE AND EDUCATE THE RIGHT PUPPY FOR YOU

puppy handbook

HOW TO CHOOSE AND EDUCATE THE RIGHT PUPPY FOR YOU

Gwen Bailey

Collins

AUTHOR'S NOTE
Throughout this book I have referred to 'he' rather than 'she'. This is just to avoid writing he/she all the time, or the rather impersonal 'it'.

First published in hardback as *The Ideal Puppy* in 2000 by HarperCollins*Publishers*, London

First published in paperback in 2002 by Collins, an imprint of HarperCollins*Publishers*
77-85 Fulham Palace Road
Hammersmith, London W6 8JB

Collins is a registered trademark of HarperCollins Publishers Limited

The Collins website a

07 06 05

9 8 7 6 5

© HarperCollins*Pub*
© Photographs: Tim

Gwen Bailey asserts
of this work.

A catalogue record for this book is available from the British Library

ISBN 0 00 714264 1

This book was created by **SP Creative Design**
Editor: Heather Thomas
Art Director: Rolando Ugolini

Photography:
The Blue Cross: pages 19 and 30
David Dalton: pages 50, 55, 56, 72, 79, 85, 94 (top), 123, 124
Tim Ridley: Cover and pages: 3, 7, 10, 12, 13, 14, 15, 18, 24, 25, 26, 31, 32, 33, 34, 35, 36, 37, 38, 39, 40, 41, 43, 45, 46, 47, 49, 54, 56, 66, 74, 80, 94 (bottom), 101 and 126
Bruce Tanner: pages 1, 9, 16, 17, 23, 27, 29, 44, 48, 51, 52, 57, 59, 61, 63, 64, 65, 67, 68, 69, 70, 71, 73, 75, 76, 77, 78, 81, 83, 84, 86, 87, 88, 89, 90, 91, 93, 95, 96, 97, 99, 100, 102, 104, 105, 106, 107, 108, 109, 110, 111, 112, 113, 114, 115, 116, 117, 118, 119, 120, 121, 122, 125, 127 and 128
Rolando Ugolini: pages 6, 8, 11, 21, 22, 42, 53, 57, 58, 62, 82, 98 and 103

Colour origination by Colourscan, Singapore
Printed and bound by Printing Express Ltd, Hong Kong

Contents

INTRODUCTION

Watching a puppy grow and develop is a pleasure that happens only occasionally in the course of an ordinary lifetime. It can be a daunting moment when you realise that the responsibility of how your puppy will turn out, how friendly it will be, and how well-behaved, lies with you. This book attempts to arm you with the knowledge you will need to ensure that your puppy grows into a well-balanced, obedient, sociable adult dog.

Puppies come in all shapes, sizes and characters and this book also endeavours to help you choose a dog that will be right for you and your family, or to help you make the most of the type of puppy you have if you have already obtained one.

All of the techniques and exercises in this book are based on positive, reward-based ideas, rather than on punishment for bad behaviour. Puppies, like children, do need to be clearly taught what is and is not acceptable, but this can be done gently and effectively without the use of force.

You are likely to receive a lot of advice from a variety of sources when you have a puppy and you will need to decide for yourself what is useful and what is not. Try not to listen to the loudest voice, which may not always be saying the right thing. Instead think hard about what is really best for your puppy and its education. Good luck and I hope that your puppy turns out to be a friendly, happy dog that you are proud to call your own.

CHOOSING A PUPPY

1

Raising a puppy is fun and can be one of life's most rewarding experiences. Time and care taken during the first year to educate and mould your puppy into an ideal adult will be well rewarded. This book will give you the tips and instructions that are often sadly lacking when a puppy is acquired. The information given is based on tried and tested techniques and uses positive methods throughout, rather than punishment, to ensure that your puppy grows up to be friendly rather than fearful.

Before beginning the education of a young puppy, a careful choice of the raw material is essential. Choosing a puppy with the right genetic make-up is not difficult but it will help to avoid disappointment as your puppy grows into an adult. Not only will it make the job of raising your puppy easier but it will also increase the likelihood that you end up with a dog that is right for you and your family. Carefully selecting not only the breed but also the strain or line from which your puppy comes will help to ensure success.

BREED CHARACTERISTICS

Throughout the book, there are references to the breeds of dog that are the most popular. The characteristics of dogs of these breeds are explored and some indication is given as to which breeds would be right for different types of

BELOW: *It is easy to fall in love with a puppy so think carefully about which breed of dog would suit you BEFORE you begin to visit breeders.*

owner. However, this is only meant to be a guide and is based on my experience of the overall characteristics of the different breeds and the people who usually own them successfully. There will always be exceptions to every rule and this is particularly true for anything related to animals.

MONGRELS AND CROSSBREDS

When considering which puppy to choose, it is important not to forget the mongrel (a mixture of a number of breeds), or crossbred (usually the first cross from two pure-bred dogs). These dogs have an intrinsic value of their own with characteristics too numerous to mention here. Their individuality makes each of them unique and they are renowned for having a more healthy constitution than pedigree dogs due to a lack of inherited problems, which are displayed by many pure-bred dogs, coming from a smaller gene pool.

TEMPERAMENT AND LIFESTYLE

When attempting to choose the right type of dog for you, you should consider the temperament of the people in your family and also the kind of lifestyle you will want your dog to lead.

Firstly, finding a dog that will be just right for you will depend on your own personality type and that of other family members. Are you very gentle with animals or the sort of person who will take a 'no-nonsense' approach? Do you always give in to demands or do you like to get your own way? Matching your character to that of your dog can save a lot of problems later. Are you fun-loving or quite

ABOVE: *A dog is for life, not just for the present so always take time over choosing your puppy.*

PUPPY NOTES

Although the photographs in this book are mostly of pedigree dogs, mongrels and crossbreds are just as valuable as family pets.

sedate? Do you want a very close bond with your dog or would you prefer to be more independent? Are you loud and boisterous, or quiet and gentle? Thinking about your own personality will help you to choose a puppy that will grow into an adult that suits you. Throughout this book, examples are given of successful owner/puppy combinations. To get further information on breed characteristics, look in breed books or ask people who already own a dog of the breed of your choice.

LEFT: *Are you quite energetic or a couch-potato? Matching your own exercise requirements to that of an adult dog is an essential task before choosing a puppy.*

In addition to considering what type of puppy personality you need, you should also consider your dog's likely lifestyle as an adult. Are you, for example, a sociable family which needs a dog that will be good with visitors, or do you live in an area where you prefer your dog to be suspicious of strangers? Do you like to go on long, energetic walks or runs, or are you one of a family of couch-potatoes? Will your dog be taken everywhere with you, or is it likely to be left at home for long periods?

BELOW: *Are you fun-loving or are you quite sedate? Springer Spaniels usually fit in well with happy, fun-loving families.*

Taking your own temperament and lifestyle into account when choosing the type of puppy you require will make it much more likely that you will end up with an adult dog that you will enjoy and that will be right for you.

11

SOCIALIZATION

This is the process by which puppies learn how to be
sociable with other animals. Puppies kept only with
other dogs for the first six months of their life will reserve
all their social behaviour for other dogs and will act like
wild animals when faced with a human. For this reason, it
is essential that the process of socialization with people is
carried out well and thoroughly while the puppy is still very
young if it is to grow into a successful pet dog.

As well as people, it is essential for a puppy to be well
socialized with its own kind so that it remains friendly and
interactive with other dogs it meets. In addition, puppies
should be socialized with other animals that we keep as
pets, such as cats, rabbits, hamsters and small birds.

As well as socializing with people and other animals,
it is also essential that a young puppy becomes familiar with

BELOW: *The result of a lack of
early socialization. Despite a
caring owner, this dog remains
afraid and is reluctant to approach
or be friendly with strangers.*

all the sights, smells, sounds and events that are part of our everyday life. Puppies need to become familiar and comfortable with all household events, such as visitors arriving, vacuuming, dustbin collection and the telephone ringing, if they are to live easily as pets in our homes. They also need to get used to a wide variety of everyday experiences, such as bus or car travel, walks in the town and country, and visits to the vet.

WHY IS SOCIALIZATION SO IMPORTANT?

Shy dogs are often less successful as pets since they are not as friendly with strangers and are not happy when taken out and about. Dogs that are not socialized with people will be scared of them and worried when they approach. This fear can rapidly develop into aggression. Dogs that have not been well socialized as puppies with other dogs will not have the social skills necessary for successful encounters with them, and may get into fights more often.

A puppy that has only a limited access to home life and to the outside world will be on edge and frightened when it is taken to new places. Outings with shy dogs are likely to be a trial for both the dog and its owner.

ABOVE: *Young puppies need to be protected from contagious diseases until fully vaccinated. Until then, they can be carried in areas that may have been soiled by other unvaccinated dogs.*

LEFT: *Getting to know about the big, wide world in which humans live is very important if a puppy is to grow up to be confident in all everyday situations.*

WHEN SHOULD SOCIALIZATION BEGIN?

A puppy's senses begin to operate at the age of about three weeks. Gradually it begins to take in information about the world around it. Up until the age of about twelve weeks, it will be relatively fearless, but after this time, it becomes increasingly wary of things that are new to it. For this reason, the ideal time to socialize a puppy is between three and twelve weeks of age when it will take new things in its stride and will rapidly become confident and outgoing. Familiarization with humans, other animals and things in the environment should then continue until the puppy is one year old so that all the good early work can be maximized.

If a puppy has missed out on early socialization, it is possible to make up for lost time, but this becomes increasingly difficult as the puppy gets older. Such puppies may always remain shy in certain situations.

BELOW: Socialization with adults and children should begin early and continue throughout your puppy's development. It is one of the most essential processes for a pet dog.

WHAT YOU NEED TO DO

It is important that you acquire a puppy from a breeder who has taken care to rear their puppies in a home environment and who has made every effort to maximize their development (see page 16). Once you get your puppy home, you will need to implement a gradually increasing schedule of events that are designed to give him good exposure to people, other animals and environments.

Socializing a puppy and taking him out and

about to experience new situations is not difficult, but it does require a sustained effort while he is young. It is easy to let a week go by because you are too busy, but you will never get such a good opportunity again to make your puppy confident and friendly. Try to do something different with your puppy each day and ensure that he meets at least one new adult or child and has a good experience with them.

Take care not to overwhelm him with too much too soon. Watch your puppy to see whether he is enjoying new events and taking everything in his stride. If he is looking worried or anxious, slow down and let him take time to overcome his concerns. Do a small amount several times each day so that he does not become tired. Gradually, as your puppy grows, you will be able to do more each day and can begin to include him in your daily life more easily instead of making special preparations just for him.

It is important that a young puppy is protected from disease since their immune system will not be as efficient as it will be later in life. For this reason, it may be necessary to carry your puppy in order to avoid unvaccinated dogs or areas where they may have soiled. Talk to your veterinary surgeon about the best way to protect your puppy and take your puppy out and about safely as soon as he has settled into your home. In this way, he will grow into a happy, friendly dog which is confident with new people or other dogs and is able to encounter new situations and cope with unusual events without worry.

TOP: *Socialization also needs to take place with other animals that your puppy may encounter in later life.*

ABOVE: *During any introductions, ensure that the puppy cannot follow his natural instincts and chase the other animals.*

15

BELOW: *There is more stimulation, more to get used to, and more visitors and activity in a household than in a kennel.*

THE IDEAL BREEDER

A good breeder will always do the following things. Check them out before buying a puppy.

■ Select suitable parents from genetic lines known to produce puppies with a good temperament and lack of inherited defects.

■ Ensure that the puppies and their mother are kept healthy and stress-free.

■ Begin the socialization process by ensuring that puppies meet and have many pleasant encounters with humans of different ages, other dogs and pets from a very early age.

■ Raise the puppies in a household environment where they can get used to everyday sounds, sights, smells and events.

■ Provide a succession of objects for the puppies to play with and explore.

■ Make sure that the puppies are able to move away from

the nest area to eliminate. This will help to ensure that the puppies are very easy to house-train (see page 44).

It is best to find a breeder who has done all of the things listed above. Try not to be tempted to buy a sick-looking puppy that has been kept in a barn for all of its short life with no special attention. You may help that puppy, but if the breeder can make money with such a careless approach, he or she will be encouraged to do it again, and, long-term, you will be adding to the misery inflicted on dogs by such people.

ABOVE: *Having puppies to protect does tend to heighten any aggressive tendencies in bitches. This dog is relaxed with visitors and the new owners can see that she has a good temperament.*

Insist on seeing the mother with the puppies to ensure that they are definitely her offspring. This will allow you to judge her temperament. Be wary if the breeder says that she is a bit protective of them. This is quite natural, but she should not be so worried about visitors that she has to be put outside while you view her puppies. Be very suspicious if the mother cannot be viewed for some reason. If the breeder says she is out for a walk, ask to return later so that you can see her. If the mother shows any signs of aggression towards you, look elsewhere for a puppy.

WHERE TO GET A GOOD PUPPY

It's not always easy to find a good breeder, but the time you spend searching is very worthwhile. One of the best ways is to find the breeder of an adult dog that you like, and contact them to see if they are likely to breed any more puppies from

RIGHT: *If you are able to get to know other dogs with similar breeding lines, you will get a good indication of how your puppy can develop.*

the same lines. By doing this, you will be able to see what temperament and characteristics are likely to be produced, which is a lot safer than launching into the unknown.

DOG SHOWS AND TRAINING CLASSES

If you do not know any dogs of your chosen breed, it may be worth visiting dog shows and training classes and talking to the owners of the dogs that interest you. If you investigate thoroughly enough, you should be able to determine which lines or strains in the breed you should steer clear of and which may be a likely prospect.

LOCAL NEWSPAPERS

Advertisements in local papers or specialist papers carrying only items for sale are a less reliable source of a good puppy. All too often, these advertisements are placed by owners of puppy farms or by dealers, or by people whose only motivation is to make money by breeding dogs. They are likely to be

18

unconcerned about their future temperament or inherited diseases and health problems since these will materialize long after the deal is done. Some advertisers cleverly disguise the fact that their puppies have been bred in very poor conditions and transported to the place of sale. Ask to see the mother with the puppies, check that the address on the pedigree papers fits that of the address you go to and trust your instincts to tell you whether anything is amiss.

ABOVE: *A reputable animal welfare charity, such as The Blue Cross, will do all it can to ensure that their puppies are in good physical and emotional health before they go to their new home.*

ANIMAL WELFARE CHARITIES

A good place to obtain a non-pedigree puppy is one of the more reputable animal welfare charities. Try to make sure that the staff have socialized the puppies thoroughly and have taken steps to make up for the fact that they have not been living in a home environment or may have needed to make up for lost time.

PUPPY FARMS

Puppy farming is a trade that does no favours for the dogs or their owners. Mothers and puppies are often kept in appalling conditions and the puppies taken away too young and transported via a 'middleman' to a holding facility before finally being sold on to an unsuspecting owner. Puppies from puppy farms are often unhealthy, develop inherited problems later on and are often very traumatised by their early life, resulting in strange behaviour or a difficult temperament. Puppy farm outlets often have litters of several different breeds for sale at any one time. Alternatively, the middlemen may try to disguise the fact that their stock comes from puppy farms by arranging to deliver the puppy direct to you, or trying to pass off the puppies as being from a bitch they own that is completely unrelated.

19

WHICH PUPPY?

If you want a bold puppy which will have a strong character but which may prove to be a bit of a handful, then choose the one in the litter that comes straight up to you. However, if you want a puppy that may be a little more reserved, choose one that is more cautious. A puppy that does not march straight over to you, but comes over quite quickly after weighing up the situation, may be easier to control and more willing to do as you ask. If you want a dog that is suspicious of anything new, or is shy with anyone outside the immediate family but will develop a very strong attachment to you, you should choose the puppy that is most reluctant to interact with you.

AT WHAT AGE SHOULD A PUPPY BE TAKEN HOME?

The best age to take a puppy home is at about six to seven weeks. By this age, it will have spent enough time learning social skills from its mother and littermates and should be robust enough to begin life in a household full of humans. If you leave it any later than nine weeks, the puppy will get less of the vital one-to-one interaction with humans that will help to ensure it grows up friendly and confident. An exception to this is where the breeder or rescue shelter has taken time and care with each puppy on an individual basis.

ARE YOU A SUITABLE OWNER?

A good breeder will want to ensure that you will be a suitable owner. Answer questions honestly and try not to be too offended if a breeder genuinely feels that you would be better off with a different breed.

Pedigree breeders often run on puppies until they are about six months old to see which one will have the best conformation for showing. Do not be tempted to take an older puppy that has not lived as a pet dog in a busy household. Such dogs often find it very difficult to adjust to normal family life.

ONE OR TWO?

Do not be tempted to take two puppies from the same litter, no matter how appealing or how ever hard the breeder tries to sell them. Puppies that grow up together will form a very strong bond with each other. As a result, they are likely to be less obedient, less attached to their owners and more unruly than dogs that are raised singly.

LEFT: *Never be tempted to take home two puppies from the same litter. It would be much better if each grew up to be a pet dog that learns to prefer the company of humans to other dogs.*

SOCIABLE PUPPIES

2

D ogs that really enjoy being with people make the best pets for sociable owners. Whether a dog will be sociable or not depends on the following:

■ Its genetic make-up.

■ Its upbringing, including the amount of socialization it receives, and the environment in which it lives.

A puppy that has parents and ancestors that were good-natured and friendly will be easier to socialize and raise than a puppy which had aggressive or fearful parents. Puppies whose genetic make-up is poor will be more difficult to socialize and are likely to be predisposed to

PUPPY FACT

A puppy's adult character and behaviour is dependent on *both* genetic make-up and upbringing.

LEFT: *Gundogs like to hold objects in their mouths and they are usually enthusiastic toy players.*

being afraid, shy or aggressive. Puppies like this can turn out all right but will take up more of your time and are more likely to do so in expert hands.

Even if its genes predispose a dog to be friendly and unafraid, good behaviour is not guaranteed unless the puppy is raised well. Of all the influences on future behaviour, socialization and upbringing have the biggest effect. Being raised with care, with plenty of social contact and exposure to the world in which we live will usually turn most puppies into happy, friendly adults.

As well as a good socialization and upbringing, how a dog lives as an adult will also have an effect on its behaviour. A dog that finds itself in a hostile world with aggressive, nasty owners will rapidly develop strategies for coping and its behaviour will deteriorate as a result. Similarly, shy, unfriendly dogs kept in a happy safe environment will usually change their behaviour and become better pets.

BELOW: Dogs that are friendly will enjoy life more and will be more rewarding for their owners.

24

PUPPIES FOR FAMILIES WITH CHILDREN AND TEENAGERS

If your dog is to live with children or have frequent contact with them, it is particularly important that you choose the right puppy at the beginning. A puppy that has been bred to be good-natured and which has been well socialized and brought up with children has the best chance of being friendly with them as an adult.

For families with young children, dogs from breeds in the Gundog group (see page 26) may be most suitable. These dogs have been bred to work closely with people and to be biddable and trainable. Of all groups, the Gundog group possesses dogs with the most friendly of natures and this may explain their popularity with owners.

BELOW: A placid, steady dog with a soft mouth is ideal for families with very young children.

FAMILIES WITH TODDLERS

Puppies need a lot of time and attention and, for this reason, it is not advisable to take on a new puppy if you have babies or several very young children. If you have very young children, and have enough free time to raise a puppy, one of the more placid breeds, such as the Golden Retriever, may be a good choice. Obviously, it will depend where the puppy comes from, but, if the breeding is good, this may be one of the best options for families with very young children.

FAMILIES WITH SCHOOL-AGE CHILDREN

These families need a robust, active dog that will be good with visiting children as well as those in the family. Labrador Retrievers often make ideal dogs for these conditions which helps to explain why they are the most popular breed of dog in both the United Kingdom and the United States. As with all puppies,

RIGHT: *Labradors usually make good companions for families with school-age children which helps to explain their consistent popularity as pets.*

the experiences the puppy has with children early on, both in the litter and in the new home, will set the scene for his future behaviour. If all experiences with children of all ages are pleasant, non-frightening and fun, the puppy is likely to grow up to be tolerant of their attentions and to enjoy their company. School-age children and their friends are likely to want to play with their dog and members of the Gundog group are usually great toy players. Any problems experienced with Labradors are likely to be those of over-exuberance, such as jumping up or play-biting and chewing since they have been bred to enjoy using their mouths.

FAMILIES WITH TEENAGERS

For families with teenagers, it is less crucial that the puppy acquired has 'safe' genetics since teenagers are more adult in their behaviour and are therefore less likely to interact inappropriately. Teenagers are often more interested in life outside the home and are likely to quickly lose interest in a new puppy once the novelty has worn off. However, they will often still expect their pets to take an interest in them and their friends from time to time, but these moments are likely to be rare. Dogs that will cope quite well with this are those of a more independent nature who also have a strong character of their own. Staffordshire Bull Terriers and Beagles fall into this category and thus would make good pets for a family with older children.

RIGHT: *Dogs with a strong, independent nature, such as Staffordshire Bull Terriers, usually make good pets for teenagers.*

27

FIRST INTRODUCTIONS

Introducing your new puppy to other family members should be done gradually so that he is not overwhelmed with too much too soon. When you first bring your puppy home, stay out in the garden with him for a while and allow him to relax, go to the toilet and recover from the journey.

INTRODUCING YOUR PUPPY TO CHILDREN

Shut other pets in another room until the new puppy has had a chance to explore the house. Ask your children to sit down, either on the floor or on chairs, and allow the puppy to go to them, rather than them crowding round him. Give them each a few small food treats and a toy so that your puppy's first encounter with them is very pleasant. Keep introductions short and distract your children with a new game so that they give the puppy a chance to rest. Ensure that your puppy has an area where the children are not allowed to touch him and teach him to use this area when he needs to sleep.

MEETING OTHER DOGS

Hold on to your new puppy when introducing him to any other dogs in the family and allow them to sniff each other. Dogs that are not used to puppies often become distressed and aggressive if puppies persist in running after them or jumping on them, so prevent this if it is too much for your dog. If the introduction does not go well and either dog is very worried about the other, keep them separated, using a playpen or a stair gate, until they have got used to the sight and smell of each other.

INTRODUCING OTHER PETS

When introducing your puppy to other pets, especially cats, prevent him from giving chase or nipping as the other pet moves away. Otherwise, this can quickly lead to a bad habit, as well as making the other pet scared. Hold on to your puppy so that you can prevent him from doing anything that the other pet may not like. You will need to have many more calm introductions over a period of days before both accept each other.

BELOW: *The initial introductions to children need to be controlled so that the encounter is pleasant for all concerned.*

29

THE FIRST NIGHT

BELOW: *Your puppy
is likely to feel very
lonely on his first
night away from
his mother and
littermates. Taking
him up to your room
until he is used to
being alone can save a
lot of sleepless nights.*

Everything will seem new and strange to the puppy on the first night in his new home and he will be missing his littermates. It may be advisable to take him up to your room for the first few nights and put him on a blanket in a high-sided box from which he cannot get out. If he cries in the night, take him out into the garden to go to the toilet.

After a few days, your puppy will have got used to being on his own in his bed in the kitchen and you can

begin to leave him down there at night. Once you have decided to do this, you should ignore any noise he may make initially in an attempt to get you to go down to let him out. The only exception to this is if he wakes in the night and you think he may need to go to the toilet.

PUPPY PLAYPENS

Puppies that have the run of the house can get into all sorts of trouble and learn bad habits when you are not there to supervise them. A better option is to restrict your puppy to a puppy playpen when you are not able to concentrate on him. The pen needs to be large enough to contain a bed and have an area with toys and chews for playing. Take him out of this pen as much as possible before he becomes bored, and especially just after he has woken up so that he can be taken outside to the toilet.

ABOVE: *A puppy playpen is the ideal place for your puppy to rest while you are not able to supervise. Ensure he spends much more time out of it than in.*

Puppy playpens allow you to relax, knowing that your puppy is safe. They also help teach your puppy self-control since he cannot do what he wants all the time. Ignore your puppy when he barks or tries other ways to get your attention when he is in the pen, unless you think he may want to go to the toilet. Although it is convenient to keep your puppy in the pen, you must ensure that he is spending most of his time out of it learning how to behave well in the rest of the house.

31

CHEWING

BELOW: *There are many chews on the market that are suitable for puppies. Choose softer items for a very young puppy and give them harder ones as they gradually mature.*

There are two stages during which puppies are likely to do lots of chewing. These are the teething stage (from fourteen to twenty-eight weeks) and the exploratory chewing stage (from six to ten months). Most owners know about the teething stage but are unprepared for the second, more destructive chewing stage.

During teething, your puppy will need to chew to assist the process of replacing puppy teeth with adult ones. It takes up to seven months for all the adult teeth to appear, but the urge to chew is most intense in the early weeks of the puppy's life.

SUITABLE CHEWS

To prevent your puppy wanting to chew items left lying around your house, provide him with plenty of suitable things to chew and gnaw. There are lots of products on the market which may be suitable, such as rawhide chews, sterilized marrow bones, nylon bones and deep-fried bones. Anything that is edible that does not produce harmful or sharp pieces is usually suitable. Some puppies like to chew hard objects, while some can only manage softer things. Puppies like variety so try to give them something new to chew every few days. Puppies

RIGHT: *Smoked bones may not be quite as appealing as some other chews but they are clean, smell nice and do not leave unpleasant bits on the carpet.*

will also chew rubber toys but some do not find these as satisfying as things that are edible. Since toys are expensive, it is sensible to reserve these for playing and provide special chews for chewing.

LEFT: *Rawhide chews need to be replaced quite often but they are an ideal way for a puppy to exercise his jaws and reduce the discomfort of teething.*

CORRECTING YOUR PUPPY

It is important not to leave a puppy in a room with access to valuable items or things that may injure him before he has learned right from wrong. To teach him what he should and should not chew, try to make all correction for chewing the wrong thing seem to come out of the blue rather than from you.

To do this, wait until you see your puppy heading for something he wants to chew, such as the corner of a rug. Just before he settles down to put his teeth on it, throw something that will rattle when it lands beside him or squirt him just behind the ear with a water spray. You will need to tailor the surprise that your puppy gets to his sensitivity. What will surprise some puppies will frighten others. Your puppy should be sufficiently unsettled by the experience to get up and move away but not to run away in panic. Timing is important, and it is more effective to arrange for the correction to happen just before he begins to chew rather than while he is doing so.

Another important point is that he should not connect the

BELOW: *If you do not provide your puppy with a constant supply of suitable items to chew, he will resort to taking things he should not.*

correction with you. If it appears to come out of the blue, it will be more effective and will remain fixed in his mind when you are not present. Since you have not become unpleasant, he can go to you for reassurance if he feels worried. Soon after he has been 'corrected' for chewing the wrong thing, take something up to him that he should chew and praise him well for the correct behaviour.

ABOVE: *A Kong stuffed with biscuits or other appetizing items can keep a puppy occupied for a long time.*

Puppies have no sense of value for objects and you will not be able to teach them this by punishing them after the event. If your puppy has already chewed something valuable, consider it to be your fault for not supervising him properly and giving him too much freedom before he has learned right from wrong.

THE EXPLORATORY CHEWING STAGE

During the exploratory chewing stage, puppies can do a lot of damage because they are so much bigger. At six months of age, puppies will be reaching puberty and becoming adolescent. In the wild at this time, they would be beginning to disperse from the litter and would cover a wider range of territory. Making sure they have plenty of exercise and a chance to explore away from their own territory will help this stage pass more easily. Make sure that your puppy has plenty to do when you leave him alone (see page 52) and offer him lots of different and exciting things to chew on a regular basis. One way to do this is to have at least seven chews and give only one each day of the week. In this way, it will be a whole week before your puppy sees that chew again and this will help him to stay interested in it.

COPING WITH PLAY-BITING

While still in the litter, puppies will play together by grabbing each other with their mouths and holding on. When your new puppy comes into your home, he will try to do the same to you. Puppies have lots of loose skin covered with fur to protect them from bites from other puppies. However, their teeth are needle-sharp and when your puppy tries to bite you, with your thin, taut, hairless human skin, even though it is in play, it will probably hurt.

HOW TO STOP PLAY-BITING

The natural reaction for most owners is to tell their puppy off, but this will be confusing for him since he meant no harm, intending only to invite them to play. For this reason, it is better to teach him an alternative way to play with you. To do this, have a toy ready to offer him whenever you spend time with him. Choose soft toys for very young puppies as this will be more acceptable to them than hard rubber toys. If he chooses your hand instead of the toy, make a fist and keep it very still. With the other hand, move the toy fast

1 Make a fist with the hand your puppy tries to bite and keep it still. Shake the toy vigorously with the other hand.

2 Praise him when he begins to bite the toy instead and have an exciting game with him.

and erratically so that it becomes more enticing. Praise him whenever he begins to bite on the toy instead of you. Keep the game interesting by keeping the toy moving so that he does not become bored and try to bite you again.

At first, and for some time, he will still try to get you to play in the way that worked while he was still in the litter. However, gradually, he will learn how to play acceptably and the puppy mouthing will begin to subside.

Another method for stopping persistent biting at a time when you do not have a toy close by is to cry out loudly as if in pain whenever he sinks his teeth into you. (This may not be so difficult to do as it is likely that he will hurt when he bites!) This will probably make him wag his tail and try to lick you, but do not get into a situation where you shriek, he gets excited and bites harder, and you shriek more.

ABOVE: *Use a line or lead to stop persistent biters. Offer an exciting toy instead as you let him approach next time.*

CURBING PERSISTENT BITERS

For older puppies or the more persistent biters, or those that bite too hard to ignore, attach a short piece of line to the puppy's collar before you give him attention. You can then use this to draw him gently away from your hand every time he tries to bite it. Offer an exciting toy instead and, after a few sessions, he will realise that fun stops if he bites you but continues if he bites the toy.

SUPERVISE CHILDREN

It is particularly important that puppies learn not to bite children, even in fun. Young children, especially, are likely to shriek and move away rapidly when bitten, which excites the puppy and encourages him to do it again. Supervise playtimes between your puppy and children and make sure he is learning the right thing. Teach your children how to encourage the puppy to play with a toy so that he learns to bite it rather than them.

DISCOURAGING ENERGETIC PLAY-BITING

Puppies are attracted by things that move and will often run after you as you walk past them. As they gain more confidence, they may try to entice you to play by biting your ankles or hanging on to trouser legs and skirts. Play-biting of this sort needs to be discouraged at once so that your puppy learns that it is not acceptable. If it happens, stand still abruptly and shout loudly so that your puppy realises that he has made a mistake. Be frightening enough to stop him, but praise him warmly when he does so. Make sure you are playing enough games with him and giving him sufficient attention at other times so that his desire to get you to play at this time is not so strong.

RIGHT: *Do not allow a puppy to play this game, especially when he is very young. It can become a bad habit which can be difficult to stop later.*

37

GOOD MANNERS

I f your puppy does something and finds it rewarding, he
is likely to do it again. This is also true for behaviour
that you wish he would not learn, such as jumping up and
stealing food, as well as for behaviour you like. If you let
unacceptable behaviour happen during puppyhood, the
habit will be set for life and will be very difficult to break.
For this reason, it is very important to stop or prevent
problem behaviour straight away and develop good
behaviour instead.

PREVENTING PROBLEM BEHAVIOUR

*BELOW: Your puppy
will not see this as
'stealing'. Dogs are
opportunists and will
make the most of any
situation they find
themselves in.*

Think carefully about the way you want your puppy to
behave when he is an adult. Do you want him to beg for
food while you are eating, jump up, get on the bed or
furniture, pull on the lead, steal food, pester visitors, and
bark excessively? If you do not, you will need to prevent
him learning how rewarding these behaviours can be while
he is still young. Try not to let
your puppy do these things,

or stop them as soon as you see them occurring.
If you can prevent all problem behaviour from happening
while he is growing up, he will not learn how rewarding it
can be and will probably never try it when he is older.

If you are unable to prevent unwanted behaviour, stop
it as soon as it occurs. Distract your puppy so that he
stops being rewarded by the bad behaviour and show
him what you want him to do instead.

ENCOURAGING GOOD BEHAVIOUR

Try to manipulate situations while your puppy is
growing up so that it is easy for him to behave
well. If, for example, you always
bend down when greeting
your puppy and get visitors
to do the same, he will never
learn that it is necessary to
jump up to get closer to
your face. He will just wait
until you come down to him
since he will have learned that
you always do so. If you find that
he is very good when greeting you but gets too excited
when greeting children or other visitors, be ready to hold
on to his collar when he does so and try to push him down
at the moment he begins to leap up. Ask your visitors to
greet him only when he has all four feet on the ground.

Try not to make too many concessions on bad
behaviour just because your puppy is still very young. Insist,
gently, but firmly, on good manners at all times and your
puppy will quickly understand what he can and cannot do.
Make sure he is well rewarded for doing the right thing,
and slowly good habits will form that will last a lifetime.

ABOVE: *Bending down to greet your puppy will help him to realise that there is no need to jump up. Rewarding him when all four of his feet are on the ground makes it more likely that he will wait for you to come down to him next time.*

PREVENTING PROBLEMS WITH OTHER DOGS

I f dogs lived with other dogs all of their lives, they would learn the social rules and body language necessary for peaceful encounters with unfamiliar dogs. However, many pet dogs grow up with only humans in their family and thus are unprepared for meetings with others from their species. This can lead to problem encounters and fighting, especially during the adolescent period when hormone surges are affecting behaviour.

PUPPY CLASSES

ABOVE: *A well-run puppy training class is fun and educational for both the owners and their puppies.*

To avoid problems later, it is important that your puppy has the chance to play regularly with other friendly dogs as he grows up. One way to do this is to join a puppy training and socialization class. Puppies can be taken to these classes from about sixteen weeks of age onwards. Older puppies are kept out of the classes as they can be too boisterous for the young ones. A good trainer will allow only one or two selected puppies off lead at a time. This allows puppies with similar characters to play and gain confidence and prevents a free-for-all which frightens some and makes bullies of others. Puppy classes are a good place for puppies to learn the social graces of their own species.

PLAYING WITH ADULT DOGS

As well as puppy classes, it is important that your puppy has the chance to play with friendly adult dogs. If your puppy only comes into contact with other puppies, his boisterous play behaviour is likely to get him into trouble when he reaches maturity.

Adult dogs that like puppies but will not tolerate them putting their teeth and paws all over them will help to teach them respect for others. These dogs will need to have been well socialized with other dogs and be used to puppies. Finding suitable dogs can be difficult but it is well worth the effort.

If you have another dog at home, it is still important that your puppy meets other dogs and puppies. This will help him to learn how to deal with different canine characters and may prevent him from getting into fights as an adult.

ABOVE: *This adult dog makes it very clear that it does not want to play at this time. A well-socialized dog like this one will help to teach your puppy respect without being aggressive.*

LEFT: *If your puppy will not read the signs that the other dogs give, help out by physically controlling him so that he learns how to behave.*

41

GENTLE PUPPIES

3

Puppies with gentle natures need gentle, non-forceful owners. A mild-natured puppy can be intimidated and over-powered by a strong, demanding owner. In a similar way, it is important that gentle owners acquire non-forceful puppies. They are more likely to let their puppy do what it wants rather than impose their will on it, and are unlikely to respond to challenges from a forceful puppy with enough intensity to have any effect. Gentle owners who have chosen an ambitious, competitive puppy need to ensure that they apply the pack leadership rules thoroughly in order to avoid a situation where the puppy takes control (see page 60).

BELOW: Gentle owners who like to be indulgent with their dogs should always choose a puppy with a similar nature.

BREEDS FOR GENTLE OWNERS

Dogs that were bred to be companion dogs will probably be the best option for gentle owners. You could consider breeds such as the following:
- Bichon Frises
- Miniature Poodles
- Maltese Terriers
- Pomeranians

These dogs have been bred for many generations to tolerate and enjoy close contact with people. Only those with a suitable temperament as companions would have been used for breeding and this makes them a likely prospect for owners who are easygoing.

TOILET TRAINING

Nest animals have an instinctive desire to be clean and will go to the toilet outside their nest as soon as they are able. You can build on this by teaching your puppy that the whole of the house is his nest and that when he wants to go to the toilet he needs to go out into the garden.

If you have obtained your puppy from a breeder who provided both a nest and an easily accessible toileting/play area, and kept this area clean, you should find this process quite easy. If your puppy came from dirty or cramped conditions where there was no distinction between the nest and play areas, you will find it more difficult.

Different puppies learn to be clean at different rates. Gentle, easygoing puppies seem to learn more slowly than confident, strong-willed ones. Remember that a new puppy is a very young animal and it will take time for him to learn

BELOW: *These puppies will instinctively leave the nest to be clean. This is encouraged by making a clear distinction between their clean bedding and the newspaper.*

what to do and to develop enough bodily control to enable him to accomplish what is required. The more time and attention you can give him, the quicker the house-training process will be over.

AVOIDING ACCIDENTS INDOORS

You will need to be aware of what is happening with your puppy at all times so that you do not allow him to make too many mistakes indoors. To prevent him from eliminating indoors, you will need to take him outside at the following times:

- First thing in the morning (immediately, not after, you have put the kettle on!).
- After he has eaten.
- When he wakes up from a nap.
- After play.
- After any excitement (e.g. a member of the family returning home).

EVERY TWO HOURS

It is not enough to just put your puppy outside by himself. If you do this, he will try to get back inside with you and will not relax enough. You need to go out with him even if it is cold and wet, and wait until he goes to the toilet. Activity and sniffing both seem to stimulate a puppy to go. When he begins, praise him quietly. When he has finished, offer a small, tasty titbit and praise him enthusiastically.

If you follow this practice, there should be no need for your puppy to make a mistake indoors. However, life cannot always revolve around a puppy and the odd accident is bound to happen. If you see your puppy showing signs of wanting to go in the house (i.e. sniffing the ground, circling, squatting), run to the door and call him, encouraging him

ABOVE: *Always go outside with your puppy when he needs to go to the toilet. This will help him to learn more quickly. Otherwise he will spend all his time anxiously trying to get back inside with you and will probably go on the carpet once you have let him in.*

ABOVE: *Sniffing seems to speed up the process of going to the toilet and is necessary for selecting the right spot to go.*

BELOW: *As soon as your puppy begins, praise him quietly. Feed him a titbit afterwards and praise enthusiastically.*

to follow you out of the house. If he has already started, shout loudly enough to stop him and, again, run to the door, encouraging him to follow. Go out with him and follow the usual procedure. Clean up any soiled areas with a solution of biological washing powder to remove the smell that may otherwise attract him back to the same spot.

At night, when you have to go out or when you cannot concentrate on your puppy, confine him to a playpen with a nest area and a large area covered with newspaper so he can go on this if he needs to.

Gradually, he will begin to prefer to go outside rather than in the house and he will try to wait until this is possible. Watch for any small signs that he needs to go, such as running to the back door, and reward him immediately by running into the garden with him. It takes time for some puppies to be able to last out all night, so don't expect too much until he is at least six months old. Always provide newspaper at night so that he does not have to go directly on the floor.

If you live in a house with no garden, toilet training is more difficult but not impossible. Decide on a special area close to the house where you will want your puppy to go and cover this area in a material that is easily cleaned (e.g. cat litter). Begin with a large area at first so that you do not need to restrict your puppy's movement too much, and gradually reduce the area as he learns more control.

ELDERLY OWNERS

Elderly owners often need a dog that is not too energetic and can adapt to a quiet life with set routines. Puppies that have amiable, gentle characters are often the best choice, and breeds such as the Cavalier King Charles Spaniel fit this role well.

All puppies are energetic during the early years, but small dogs can have their daily exercise supplemented by games with toys in the house if necessary. This is useful for owners with limited mobility who can only manage a short walk but have plenty of time to devise games and activities that use up their puppy's energy without wasting too much of their own.

Another advantage of small size is that during the early months, when puppies are boisterous and clumsy, they are less likely to accidentally knock their owners over or injure them by jumping up as a large puppy might. Puppies of smaller breeds usually move faster than those of larger breeds and are, therefore, more likely to avoid tripping up their owners.

It is important for elderly owners to ensure that their puppy is well socialized and has learned to be left alone. Although they may lead a quiet life and may be with their puppy most of the time, this cannot necessarily continue throughout their dog's life. Raising a dog that is sociable and can cope with being left alone will help relatives if they need to look after it in later life – for example, if the owner needs an extended period in hospital.

ABOVE: *Cavalier King Charles Spaniels are ideal for owners who want companionship but who do not lead an active lifestyle.*

47

BELOW: *Giving periods of 'time out' will result in a dog that is content to leave you in peace sometimes rather than one that will constantly demand your attention.*

COPING WITH ATTENTION SEEKING

Some owners spend more time with their dogs and this encourages a closer bond. Such dogs tend to be the centre of their owner's attention most of the time and it can come as quite a surprise to them when, for example, visitors arrive or the owner answers the telephone, and they find themselves temporarily dismissed. A whole range of unwanted behaviour, such as barking, chewing, and biting or scratching the owner, may then be displayed to try to return things to normal.

If you usually devote a lot of attention to your puppy, you will need to make sure this does not happen. To achieve this, you should give your puppy regular periods of 'time out'. This means setting aside at least half an hour daily when you are in the same room as your puppy but, during this time, you should not look at, talk to, touch or speak to him. If he begins to do something you do not want, physically prevent him but with as little contact as possible. Do not allow him to sit on you or lie down touching you at these times. Stand up and move away instead. In this way, he will learn to cope without you at times when you are busy with more important things.

CAR TRAVEL AND PUBLIC TRANSPORT

Getting a puppy used to travelling in the car and on public transport is a wise precaution even if you do not need to travel often. Acclimatizing a puppy to a moving vehicle is relatively easy, but taking an adult dog in a car or on a train for the first time can be terrifying for him and traumatic for you.

While your puppy is still very young, try to take him out as often as possible for very short car journeys. Provide a comfortable, non-slip bed and drive carefully to ensure that he is not thrown about unnecessarily. Some small puppies may be better off inside a strong, securely placed box so that they can lean against the sides if necessary. Try to imagine what it must be like for a small puppy that finds itself on an erratically moving platform inside a metal box that makes a very loud noise. If you begin when your puppy is young enough, and take things at a pace that he can cope with, he will soon begin to accept, and even enjoy, car journeys.

As part of your puppy's overall education, it is helpful to take him on public transport. You may need to make a special effort to do this, but it is fun to do and will be good for your puppy. Again, try to think what the experience is like for your puppy and be careful not to let him become frightened or overwhelmed by the new surroundings and all the unfamiliar people around him.

ABOVE: *If the early journeys in the car are pleasant and not frightening, your puppy will soon accept car travel as part of life. Don't just use the car to take him to the vet!*

49

OWNERS WHO LIVE ALONE

P eople who live alone with their dog often develop a very close bond with it but cannot be there all the time. They need a dog that can withstand being in a very close one-to-one relationship most of the time, but one that can also cope with periods of isolation. Dogs of breeds that are bred to work independently but which have recently been bred as companions, such as the Yorkshire Terrier, are ideal. Dogs with this stronger type of character will also be better able to cope with long periods spent with their owners followed by a sudden need to be sociable when visitors arrive.

If you live alone, it is important that you acclimatize your puppy to being left by himself as soon as you get your puppy home (see page 52). Taking your puppy everywhere with you and then trying to leave him behind later will cause him much distress. Owners who live alone will also need to make a special effort to ensure that their puppy is socialized well with many different types and ages of people.

LEFT: *Yorkshire Terriers make ideal companions. If raised correctly, they will have enough independence to be able to cope alone when their owner is out.*

ALONE AT HOME

It is vital for all puppies to learn to tolerate isolation as it is not something that comes easily or naturally to them. Dogs have evolved from animals that were safer in a pack, and evolution has equipped them with a strong desire to want to be with others. As owners, we cannot always be with them, and it is essential that they learn to cope when left alone from an early age. This is particularly important in a household where people are at home all the time, such as owners who are retired or have families with young children. It is also important for gentle, sweet-natured puppies that seem to be particularly prone to developing separation-related problems.

LEFT: *All puppies need to be taught to be alone, especially those that live in families where they are rarely, if ever, left on their own.*

GET YOUR PUPPY USED TO BEING ALONE

BELOW: Always leave something suitable to chew when you leave your puppy at home alone. If you do not do this, or if you leave him for too long, you can expect to come back to some unwanted damage.

Begin as soon as your puppy has had a chance to settle into his new routine. Wait until he is tired and ready for a sleep. Put him in his playpen with a comfortable, warm bed, and leave the room. Ignore any of his attempts to get you to go back to him. Wait until he is asleep and try to ensure that you are around when he wakes up so that you can take him outside immediately to go to the toilet.

As he grows, gradually increase the time that he is left alone until, at about six months old, he is being left for about two hours each day. If you find, at any time during this process, that he is becoming distressed when you go out, leave him for shorter periods but more frequently. Gradually, he will begin to perceive isolation as part of life and will learn to tolerate it.

Never scold or punish a dog for what he has done while you have been away. He will not be able to learn from this. He may appear to look 'guilty' but he is simply showing submission in response to your angry mood.

If you want your puppy to get used to being left in other situations, such as at friends' houses, or in the car, begin to teach him in the same way as soon as possible.

LEAVE SOMETHING TO CHEW

OPPOSITE: Puppies can get into all sorts of mischief when left alone. Ensure that they are not left with items that they can damage, or which could harm them.

Always ensure that your puppy has enough suitable items to chew when he is left alone (see page 32). If he refuses food or chews when left, it is probably because he is too worried. If this is the case, you will need to work harder to get him used to being left alone.

PUPPY FACT

Young puppies have to learn that they cannot do what they want to do all the time. Handling exercises are a very good way to teach them that you are in control and that they must do what you want them to do until you let them go.

HANDLING AND GROOMING

Dogs do not like to hold and hug each other unless they are fighting or mating. As humans, we like to touch and hold our dogs to show our affection. Puppies need to be exposed to this from a very early age to prevent them from being worried by this later. You should begin to teach your puppy to accept being restrained as soon as he has settled in. Do this often throughout the day, gently holding, cuddling and talking to him and not letting him go until he has stopped trying to get away. When he relaxes, praise him and let him go. Do not always lift him off his feet as this can be unsettling and he may begin to avoid you. Teach him to accept being lifted up occasionally and also how to stand quietly on a table.

Accustom him early on to all the things that you or your veterinary surgeon may want to do to him at a later

LEFT: *Get your puppy used to being restrained from an early age. Hold him gently but firmly if he struggles and only let him go when he has completely accepted being held by you.*

LEFT: *When lifting your puppy, make sure that you support his weight with a hand underneath his bottom. If he feels secure, he will be much less likely to struggle.*

PUPPY FACT

Puppies that get used to being held when small will think that we are much stronger than them all their lives, even if they grow to an enormous size and strength.

date. For instance, you should teach him to accept nail clipping, teeth inspection and cleaning, grooming and bathing. Make all of these procedures as pleasant for the puppy as possible. Hold your puppy firmly but gently so that he cannot get away and learn to avoid you. Do each new procedure very slowly at first so that he has time to get used to it and not feel afraid. Some puppies will take everything in their stride whereas others will need more time to accept things being done to them by their owners.

RIGHT: *Groom your puppy every day even if he does not need it. It is a good way to allow you to do a quick health check and will help to teach him to cope with sitting still when he wants to do something else.*

LEFT: *Look in the ears while holding the head still and practise wiping the outer edges with a tissue. Exercises like this make life much easier should you ever need to give your dog medication for an ear condition.*

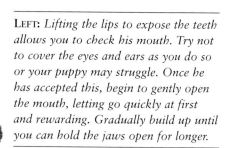

RIGHT: *When wiping your puppy's paws after a walk or bath, do so gently but firmly. Discourage any chewing of the towel or attempts to turn it into a game.*

LEFT: *Lifting the lips to expose the teeth allows you to check his mouth. Try not to cover the eyes and ears as you do so or your puppy may struggle. Once he has accepted this, begin to gently open the mouth, letting go quickly at first and rewarding. Gradually build up until you can hold the jaws open for longer.*

Put a collar on your puppy a few days after you get him and then begin to teach him to accept being restrained by it. He will accept being led on a lead more quickly if he has been used to being held by the collar, and is less likely to learn to pull.

It is very important that a puppy learns to deal with frustration from an early age. Learning that he cannot have his own way all the time and learning to cope with the feeling that arises out of this is a very important lesson. Holding your puppy when he wants to get away is one way of teaching this. Hold him gently but firmly and do not let him go until he has stopped struggling completely and has accepted the restraint.

ABOVE: *Teaching your puppy to accept being hugged or held will make him more able to tolerate it when he is older and, perhaps, a child hugs him unexpectedly.*

RIGHT: *Puppies will scratch at the collar at first because it feels unfamiliar. Ignore this; praise them when they stop and they will soon become accustomed to it.*

STRONG-WILLED PUPPIES

4

Some puppies have strong characters and will have a more forceful nature than others. Puppies with a strong character will be more ambitious, more competitive and more determined when trying to get their own way. They will need an owner with a strong nature to control them.

Some puppies are strong willed because their parents passed on traits that make it more likely that they will be like this, whereas others will be more pushy because they have always got their own way and have won all their encounters with littermates and humans. Puppies that are larger than their littermates have often had a head start when it comes to being in control and they may use their extra size to win games, possessions and encounters. They tend to be bolder than the other pups and will often be the first ones out to greet visitors. If a puppy like this goes into a home with gentle owners who let it do as it pleases, there may be difficult situations to face later on when the puppy is older and is faced with losing for the first time.

INHERITED TRAITS

While some puppies will be particularly strong-willed, nearly all are more ambitious than we expect them to be because of the nature of their ancestors. Wolves are large animals armed with teeth that can kill a large mammal. To save them from repeatedly injuring each other, a very structured hierarchical system evolved with alpha wolves at the top and the rest in an order below them. In a wolf pack, only the animals at the top of the hierarchy will breed and pass their genes on to the next generation. In addition, the alpha wolves get all the privileges, such as the best place to sleep. This is a strong motivator to be ambitious and to try to win the top spot.

Since our pet dogs are descended from wolves, the desire to be ambitious and to try to climb higher up the hierarchy has been handed down to them. Fortunately, in the process of domestication, we have weakened this desire by breeding only from the more biddable dogs. However, it is still present, although more so in some dogs than others. Since you will not always know the strength of your dog's character until he is older, it is best to assume that he may be ambitious and put in place specific measures to keep him well down in the human hierarchy from the outset.

TAKING THE LEAD

To be a good pack leader, it is necessary to adopt the attitude that, most of the time, what you want is more important than what your puppy wants. This does not mean that you should ignore his needs, as a good pack leader will always ensure that all members of the pack are comfortable and happy. Instead, it is about insisting that

PUPPY FACT

Dogs bred to work, especially those bred as guards, are usually more ambitious and strong willed than those bred as companions.

you know best and making sure that you get your own way.

This does not mean that you should bully your puppy and use aggression. On the contrary, good pack leaders rarely need to resort to such drastic action. However, they do make it clear that when they choose a certain course of action, the lower members of the pack must comply. It is often about taking care of the small things, such as insisting on good manners when visitors arrive or making a puppy move out of the way when you need to walk through a doorway. If you ask your puppy to do lots of little things that are important to you, and insist that he does them even

LEFT: *Insisting on good manners, for instance, when visitors arrive, will help your puppy to realise that his needs do not always come before yours.*

if there is resistance, it is likely that he will not dare to challenge you over issues that are more important to him.

THINGS THAT ARE IMPORTANT TO YOUR PUPPY

Your puppy lives in a less sophisticated world than our's and the things that are important to him will be different. Resting places, food, toys and getting attention from his friends will be the things that your puppy finds most important in life. If you have an ambitious puppy, taking control of these elements of his life can have the effect of raising your status. The following ideas may be useful if you have a gentle nature and a strong-willed puppy, or if you feel that you are losing control at any time. They can be implemented at any period during your puppy's

BELOW: *Make it clear that you own the territory and that he cannot always go where he wants to.*

development, and the
very same ideas can be
implemented in reverse if
you need to boost your
puppy's confidence.

OWN THE TERRITORY

Keep your puppy out of
the bedrooms and off the
furniture. Sometimes
move him from the place
where he was resting and
sit there yourself. Move
him out of the way if he is
blocking a doorway and
ensure that he waits for you to go through doorways before
him. Make sure that you take control when visitors arrive.

ABOVE: *Try not to
give attention when
you have settled down
to do something else.*

EAT FIRST

Feed your puppy after you have eaten your own meals.
It may seem like a small point to us, but food is necessary
to survival and control of it is important.

BE POSSESSIVE

Win more games of tug-of-war than you lose and take the
toy away with you at the end of the game. Leave toys down
for him to play with, but remove them if he begins to hoard
them in his bed and growls when you go near.

BE ALOOF

Pack leaders do not always respond to demands for
attention. Be aloof sometimes when you are busy with
something else. Only give him attention on your terms,
when you want to, for as long as you want to.

63

RIGHT: Not allowing a puppy to do what he wants all the time will teach him to respect what you want to do. Later, let him do what he wanted as a reward for behaving well.

NEVER MAKE A REQUEST YOU CANNOT ENFORCE

Before you ask your puppy to do something, make sure that you are in a position to back up the request with action if he does not understand or does not want to comply. If you ask him to do something and let it go when he does not, your puppy will never learn what it is you want and will learn to ignore you. If he did know what was required, but ignored you anyway, you will have lost an encounter and this will lower your status in the eyes of your puppy.

DOGS FOR STRONG-WILLED OWNERS

Dogs of some breeds, such as those that were developed partially or completely for guarding purposes, like the Dobermann and Rottweiler, are likely to be more strong willed than others. If you have a strong character and are likely to insist on getting your own way, a dog that is naturally strong willed may suit you better than one that has a more gentle nature.

To make the matter more complicated, strength of character tends to run in certain lines and strains and so some dogs of a particular breed may be very easygoing whereas others may be very ambitious. Since the tendency to be ambitious seems to depend mostly on the parents and grandparents, it may be best to look at their temperament and at the character of any of their progeny if possible.

The positive side of strength of character is that it tends to make puppies more persistent and, hence, easier to teach. It is also likely to result in a more confident puppy that is able to learn more quickly.

PUPPY FACT

Being the leader is not about imposing your will on others all the time, but about doing it enough times so that you can – any time you want.

LEFT: *Puppies with strong characters are often able to concentrate for longer and learn lessons more quickly.*

TRAINING

R eward-based training relies on the principle that 'actions that are rewarded are likely to be repeated'. Rewards for puppies can be small, tasty titbits or games with a toy. These should always be given with praise so that the puppy learns to work not just for the reward but, ultimately, for you.

To train your puppy you need to let him know what it is you want him to do, then reward him immediately for doing it. The difficult part is helping him to understand what it is that you want him to do as he does not understand language.

YOUR BODY LANGUAGE

Puppies learn hand signals and body movements much more quickly than they learn words. This is because their natural systems of communication rely on reading body language rather than on having a vocabulary.

MAKE TRAINING FUN

Training using reward methods can, and should, begin as soon as your puppy has settled in to his new home. Keep training lessons short and make them fun for both of you.

However, a trick that works very well is to position the reward in such a way that it acts as a lure to encourage him to perform the action. Later, he will learn your body movements and gestures that go with this action and, later still, he will learn the word that is associated with it.

PUPPY TRAINING AND SOCIALIZATION CLASSES

These classes will help you with your training and also help keep your puppy sociable with other dogs (see page 40). Finding a good class can be difficult but ask your vet for a recommendation and go along to a class without your puppy to see if you like their methods before enrolling. Learning the handling skills necessary to train a puppy and getting the timing right can be difficult at first for the novice owner. Having someone to show you what to do can be very instructive and can help to prevent you making mistakes that could cause difficulties later.

BELOW: *Keep titbits small. Strangely, puppies seem to work harder and for longer for tiny pieces of food.*

THE RIGHT TITBITS

Titbits need to be small so that your puppy does not become full too soon. A piece of cheese or dried liver about the size of a pea works well. Avoid giving too much new food too quickly as it can cause diarrhoea.

COME WHEN CALLED

1 Ask a friend to hold your puppy for you and let him see and sniff a tasty titbit that you are holding.

USE DIFFERENT LOCATIONS

Puppies learn a set of associations surrounding an event, rather than just the aspect we are trying to teach. For this reason, teach your puppy each exercise in different locations with varying degrees of distraction. In this way he will eventually come to understand what you mean in a variety of different situations.

2 Run backwards a little way, stop, crouch down and call him to you. Use his name or a command (choose and then be consistent) and ask your assistant to release your puppy as soon as he hears this command.

3 As your puppy runs to you, praise him excitedly and enthusiastically to keep his attention. Keep your body language 'open' to invite him to come towards you. Hold the treat out as he comes to you but do not release it straight away. Praise him and take hold of his collar before doing so. In this way he will learn to stay with you for a little while, not just run in, grab the treat and run off.

Note: Don't pat your puppy when he comes to you, particularly around the head area. This may be unpleasant for him and may make him try to avoid your hands in future. Never reach out to grab him if he is reluctant to come to you. Instead, run away and pretend to do something more interesting so that he will follow you and become interested in you again.

69

WALK ON LEAD WITHOUT PULLING

The secret of having a dog who walks well on the lead is to never allow your puppy to move forwards when the lead is tight. Otherwise he will learn to lean into his collar and pull you wherever he wants to go. He doesn't always have to walk right beside you, but he does have to learn that pulling on the lead has the unpleasant consequence of making you stop.

1 Lure your puppy into position beside you. Do this by feeding him a little piece of titbit.

2 Begin to walk forwards at a reasonable pace and encourage your puppy to come with you. Young puppies usually have a strong desire to follow so this should not be too difficult to achieve.

3 Praise him whenever he is walking nicely beside you and offer him titbits at frequent intervals to reward the good behaviour.

4 Sooner or later, your puppy will begin to go in a different direction or at a different speed to you. Keep the lead at a fixed length by holding it into your body. Watch carefully and just before the lead goes tight, stop walking. This will bring your puppy to an abrupt stop, too.

5 Encourage him to return to your side by calling him and using a titbit as a lure. Praise him well when he is back in position and give him the titbit.

USE YOUR WEIGHT

It is important that your puppy does not learn to drag you where he wants to go. Allow him to go to the end of the lead, but no further. Balance yourself so that you use your weight to prevent him from dragging you.

71

Using a head collar

Only walk your puppy on a lead and collar when you have got time to train him in this way. At other times, when you cannot concentrate on him, get him used to wearing a head collar instead which is more effective at preventing him from pulling. You can purchase one at most reputable pet shops.

Teaching the commands

PUPPY FACT

Teaching your puppy to adopt different positions on command will make living with him easier and will expand his mind so that he is able to learn other things more easily.

To get your puppy into position, use a food lure to move his head so that his body follows. Getting your puppy into position takes time and patience at first. Once he realises that he will be rewarded for taking up certain positions, it will be easy to teach him to do so on command.

Practise getting him into the different positions as shown. When he is doing these easily, begin to exaggerate your hand movements and move them away from your puppy's head slightly so that they become hand signals. Once your puppy knows the hand signals, introduce a word for each position and begin to make your hand signals more obvious. In this way, your puppy will learn which position to adopt when he hears each word.

Sit

1 Move the titbit up and back towards his tail, keeping it just above his nose all the time.

2 Do not allow him to take the titbit until he is in the correct position. If he jumps up, the titbit is too high. If he backs up, it's not high enough or you're going too fast.

3 As your puppy's bottom touches the floor, feed the titbit and praise him well.

73

DOWN

1 From the sit position, lure your puppy's nose downwards. Let him lick and chew at the titbit to keep him interested.

2 If he stands up, lure him into a sit but do not feed the titbit. Be patient as it will take a while for him to understand what he has to do in order to get the titbit.

3 Feed the titbit and praise him well as soon as your puppy's elbows are on the ground and he has relaxed.

STAND

1 From the sit position, lure your puppy forwards with a tasty titbit.

2 Always try to keep the titbit in line with your puppy's nose and just in front of it.

3 Reward him as soon as he is on his feet. If he walks forwards, move your hand more slowly next time and feed the titbit as soon as his back end has come up.

PUPPY FACT

It does not matter if you make a mistake when using reward-based training. Simply withhold the titbit, make a fuss of your puppy and start again.

Roll over

Only try this exercise once you have mastered the 'down'.

1 Begin with your puppy in a relaxed down position on a soft surface.

2 Lure your puppy's head round. (If it is difficult to proceed further, reward him a few times in this position.)

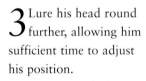

3 Lure his head round further, allowing him sufficient time to adjust his position.

4 Reward him well as he rolls over and let him know how pleased you are.

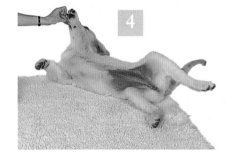

STAY

When your puppy has learnt to take up any position on command, you will be ready to teach the 'stay'.

1 Begin with your puppy sitting beside you. Ask him to stay and stand beside him. Praise him gently if he stays in position. If he moves, repeat the 'sit' command firmly.

2 If he begins to get up or tries to lie down, reposition him quickly before he has a chance to do so. Gradually increase the time he stays in place over a number of sessions (don't ask a very young puppy to stay still for too long).

3 When he is able to stay in this position for a period of time without attempting to move, repeat stage 1 but move a pace away. Reward him well for staying in position.

NOTE

Eventually you can progress to standing further away during the 'stay' and in different positions relative to your puppy.

SETTLE DOWN

The 'settle down' is a very useful exercise to teach for those times when you do not want your puppy to be up and active (such as when you go out visiting or are visited by friends who are afraid of dogs). Begin this exercise after you have taught the 'down'. Practise at a time when you are sitting down and resting.

1 Attach a lead to your puppy's collar and then ask him to lie down.

2 Roll his hips over gently until he is in a relaxed position.

3 Praise him periodically and give him a chew to gnaw on so that he has something to do.

4 Put the lead under your foot so that he cannot wander off and return him to position if he tries to get up. Keep him there for short periods at first, gradually increasing the time as he learns what is expected of him.

RIGHT: *Puppies that learn to settle down can be taken out and about to more places and may have a better life as a result.*

LITTLE DOGS WITH BIG PERSONALITIES

Dogs do not have to come from the guarding breeds to be strong willed. Many smaller breeds of dog are famous for having strong personalities, particularly the terriers. Two breeds that are often noted from their strength of character are Cocker Spaniels and West Highland White Terriers. Their sweet, gentle appearance often belies an ambitious puppy underneath, which can cause problems when they are owned by gentle-natured owners who like to spoil them.

Not all puppies of these breeds are like this, but it may be worth knowing that some are if you decide to own one. Make sure you put in place all the suggestions for keeping your puppy at the bottom of the family hierarchy (see page 62) for at least the first six months of his life. During this time, he will be assessing where his position within the family lies. If you make it very clear to him, he will accept it. If not, he is likely to be uncertain as to his position and may challenge you as he gains confidence and reaches maturity.

RIGHT: *Some dogs, even though quite small, have big personalities and will suit strong-willed owners. Such dogs may take advantage of a gentle owner's indulgence.*

PREVENTING AGGRESSION

I n the wild, competing over food and items of interest is a useful strategy to ensure that you get enough to eat. In our world, there is no need to compete in this way and it is important to teach your puppy this fact.

FOOD

All puppies should be taught that hands come to give, not take. To do this, give your puppy his dish of dinner but withhold the tasty portion if you feed fresh meat, or collect some smelly, tasty treats if you feed a complete food. Allow him to eat a few mouthfuls and then approach offering something much nicer than he has in his bowl. Do this on several occasions throughout his meal. Gradually, over several days, get closer to his bowl with your hand before allowing him to take the food. Eventually, he should welcome your hands being placed in his bowl because he learns that they will deliver something tasty.

BELOW: Teaching a puppy to enjoy having humans approach his food bowl may help to prevent a lot of problems later on.

Some puppies will have been fed communally by the breeder and may have learned to fight in order to get enough to eat. Don't punish puppies that have learned to growl over food since this only makes them worse.

CHEWS AND BONES

It is important to get your puppy accustomed to being approached when he has chews or bones. If you have difficulty with this, begin with chews that are less palatable and work up to bones. Wait until he has been chewing for some time and lure

him away from the chew with a smelly, tasty titbit. While you do this, take the chew with the other hand. After he has eaten the titbit, give him back the chew.

Toys

If your puppy is aggressive over possessions, teach him to retrieve (see page 113). Use toys at first, then other objects. Resist the temptation to chase him round and become aggressive yourself. This will only make him likely to bite when he grows up. If he is

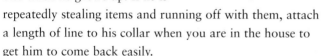

repeatedly stealing items and running off with them, attach a length of line to his collar when you are in the house to get him to come back easily.

Controlling barking

Puppies usually begin to bark when they are between six and eight months old. They may emit the occasional noise before this but a well socialized puppy should not begin to bark properly until he is more mature. Some breeds are more vocal than others. German Shepherd Dogs, some terriers and smaller breeds may be excessively vocal from an early age. You must stop this. Any habits formed during puppyhood will be very difficult to break later on.

Don't encourage your puppy to bark. Owners who do this because they want a dog that will look after the house find that they own a dog that barks excessively at the slightest noise. A well-socialized dog will bark quite naturally if he sees something suspicious on his territory and there is no need to help him to learn this.

ABOVE: *If you teach your puppy to approach you when he has a toy, rather than the other way round, he is much less likely to be possessive. Offer small titbits as a reward for letting go and he will soon be happy to give the toy up to you.*

81

PUPPIES FOR EXPERIENCED OWNERS

5

Some puppies are more difficult to raise than others and are better suited to people who have had dogs of their own before. When you own a dog, you develop the handling skills necessary to control him in difficult situations. You also acquire a knowledge of how to communicate and train dogs. This knowledge is essential when raising a puppy whose genetic make-up does not make it entirely suitable as a pet dog.

Dogs of breeds that were originally selected for such diverse occupations as killing rats and foxes, herding and guarding livestock, or chasing and killing deer or other game animals have traits that make them potentially dangerous in certain situations. Having the knowledge to play down those traits and channel their desires into acceptable outlets is important to prevent future problems. If you have had previous experience with dogs, you are much more likely to spot potential problems earlier and to know what to do when you see the warning signs than someone who has not owned dogs before.

BELOW: *Some puppies may be more difficult to raise than others and, consequently, are better suited to owners with more experience.*

83

HERDING DOGS

S hepherd dogs and collies were bred to chase livestock. Over generations, we selected those dogs that were most alert, most responsive and most interested in chasing moving objects. Finely-tuned dogs that loved to chase were perfected and then pet owners began to buy them because they liked their appearance.

Unfortunately, being raised in a pet home does not change the pre-programming. Herding dogs are still, essentially, animals bred to work and chase. We have also selected for animals that had the stamina to work all day, every day. Being raised within the confines of a pet home reduces the fitness of such animals, but does not interfere with the innate desire to exercise and use up the energy that they know they have.

BELOW: *The innate desire to give chase can cause problems later on unless you control it now and channel it in the right direction.*

Behaviour problems in herding dogs

It is not surprising that many dogs of herding breeds develop problems associated with their chase behaviour. In the absence of the real thing and any real work to do, they will turn their attentions to cars, bikes, joggers, cats and even shadows or drips of a gutter if necessary.

If you choose a puppy with this genetic make-up, it is essential that you teach him to play successfully with toys so that you can give him a 'job' to keep him occupied (see Chapter 6). It is also important that you set aside enough time every day to use up the mental and physical energy that he will have as he grows older. Fortunately, as we select more for dogs who look good, but who do not need to work, many strains or lines are losing such a strong desire to work, but it will take some time before they all have good pet dog traits instead.

ABOVE: *Unless herding dogs are given some work to do, even if it is just chasing a ball, they will find less acceptable outlets for their abilities.*

85

ABOVE: *Channelling a puppy's energy into games with toys will allow you to focus on and control his strong desire to chase.*

Dogs bred to herd animals have an alertness and responsiveness which are necessary to respond quickly to commands. With this goes a sensitivity that predisposes them to becoming afraid of things very easily. These traits make them very sensitive, loyal companions, but unless adequate socialization is carried out, it can lead to them becoming fearful, shy and aggressive. If they have a bad experience, they are likely to react adversely in the same situation long after a dog of a less sensitive nature has forgotten about it. This makes them less than ideal for loud, insensitive or angry owners who can easily send such delicate-natured animals into a downward spiral. Since the herding breeds were bred to work at some distance from their owner, they are usually very sensitive to noises and can develop noise phobias when exposed to very loud, unexpected noises.

Herding breeds are best kept by experienced, kind, energetic owners who are sensitive but not nervous themselves and willing to spend a lot of time playing with their dog and using up its physical and mental energies.

HOUNDS

Hounds were bred to hunt other animals and to work independently from humans, either singly or in a pack. They were not bred to work in close co-operation with man and are often less biddable and willing to please than other breeds. This may be the reason why they are less popular as pets and fewer are registered with The Kennel Club. In addition, they do not seem to have such a strong desire to carry and retrieve objects as other dogs and this makes them less fun to play with.

BELOW: *Hounds tend to be more aloof and less demonstrative to their owners than dogs of other breeds.*

They do, however, make ideal pets for people who want a less close relationship with their pet. Hounds tend to be slightly aloof and do not seem to need such constant reaffirmation of their bond with their owners as do other breeds. This makes them harder to train since they are not so likely to work to please you. Since they cannot be motivated easily by play either, the only motivator left is food. Fortunately, many hounds have a very large appetite and so it is possible to train them in this way!

Hounds tend to exercise in short bursts of intense activity so they are well suited to our habit of walking dogs and then having them at home for long periods. They are usually content to lie around the house, waiting until they can go out a long walk, rather than being constantly alert, looking for the next thing to do.

It is difficult to exercise hounds in areas where game, livestock or cats (or sometimes small, fluffy dogs) are present without their innate desire to chase taking over. Although you may have

87

succeeded in training them with food rewards in quiet areas, their motivation to hunt is likely to outweigh their desire to please you or to eat. Unlike the herding dogs whose desire to chase can be diverted into playing with toys, hounds prefer the real thing and there may be no alternative but to keep them on a lead in areas where they are likely to get into trouble.

ABOVE: *Hounds tend to exercise in short bursts of high energy movement.*

RIGHT: *This is followed by a long lay down to cool off!*

TERRIERS

Terriers were bred, originally, to catch and kill small animals. They were selected for their speed of reaction, tenacity and ability to work independently. These traits made them ideal for hunting and killing, but they can lead to problems in a pet dog. Luckily, terriers are often small so any problems of aggression are less severe. However, their predatory nature can cause difficulties with other small pets, such as rabbits and hamsters. Worst of all, the predatory response can lead to attacks on small babies in dogs that have not been properly socialized as puppies.

If you own a terrier puppy, make sure that he is well socialized with other animals, babies and small children from an early age (see page 14). If he comes to accept them as part of his social structure, he will be less likely to view them as potential prey later on. Some strains have more of a predatory nature than others. The amount of rough play and sustained aggression that your puppy puts into his play with squeaky toys may give you an indication of the strength of his instinct.

Terriers that are direct descendants of those bred to work are more likely to have a strong prey drive than those whose ancestors have been kept for show or as pets for many generations.

ABOVE: *Terriers usually enjoy games with squeaky toys as they simulate the noise made by captured prey.*

PREVENTING AGGRESSION

BELOW: *Puppies that meet and have fun with lots of people from an early age will be less apprehensive and less likely to bite defensively when they are older.*

Puppies will grow up into nervous adults if they are undersocialized or have enough bad experiences to make them fearful. Nervous adults are likely to bite if they feel that defence is their only option for avoiding a dangerous or painful experience. Sensitive, alert, reactive types of dog are more likely to become fearful and, hence, to turn into dogs that bite unless special care is taken to avoid this happening.

If you are starting out with a puppy, it is quite easy to ensure that he becomes a confident, friendly dog that uses defensive behaviour as an absolute last resort by doing the things listed on the following pages.

SOCIALIZE WELL

Socialize your puppy with people, including children, and other animals from an early age (see page 14). This will ensure that he

feels comfortable with the different things that people do and does not feel apprehensive when they grab him or do other unusual things to him. A well-socialized dog will accept strange behaviour from people and will take unusual occurrences in his stride and is less likely to become afraid.

ABOVE: *Use positive training methods that will reward your puppy for doing the right thing rather than punishing his bad behaviour.*

DON'T PUNISH

Dogs that are punished by their owners often view people as slightly unpredictable. Many punishments are administered to dogs for breaking rules they did not know about. All they learn from these punishments is that their owner sometimes becomes aggressive for no good reason. If, on top of this, the owner does not develop a good relationship with their pet, it is likely that the dog will view humans with slight mistrust. This leads to fear and defensive aggression when people do unusual things and can result in an unexpected bite during normal interactions with other people.

To avoid this, do not resort to punishment to get your own way. Think about how to win encounters without the

91

use of force, train your puppy using positive methods, and
teach him what you want him to do and praise and reward
him for doing so. Develop a good relationship with him,
based on trust and friendship, and he will feel comfortable
and secure in his world.

AVOID NASTY EXPERIENCES

While your puppy is growing up, try to protect him from
anything frightening or unpleasant. Experiences that cause
pain or fright can make a lasting impression and are likely
to cause dogs to become fearful when they find themselves
in a similar situation later on.

PREVENT UNPLEASANT EXPERIENCES

Accidents will happen, however, and events will take place
over which you have no control. Try to think ahead and
prevent as many of these as possible. If your puppy does
have an unpleasant experience, do not show too much
concern as this may make matters worse. Instead, be jolly
and matter-of-fact, remove him from the situation and try to
divert his attention onto something more pleasant, such as
eating titbits or games with a toy, instead. Later, when he has
calmed down, try to take him back into the same situation
again, but, this time, ensure that he has a pleasant encounter.

THE VETERINARY EXPERIENCE

A good example of all of this is what happens at veterinary
surgeries across the country. Many dogs are afraid of being
examined by a veterinary surgeon and some will try to bite
and may have to be muzzled. You will often see dogs in the
waiting room at your vet's surgery shaking, drooling and

whining with anxiety. There may be many reasons why some dogs are afraid of going to the vet, but the problem often begins during puppyhood.

Most puppies visit the veterinary surgery twice or three times for vaccinations. The injections themselves should not hurt, but the whole experience of going somewhere new, meeting other dogs in the waiting room, then being put on a table and being handled by a stranger may be totally overwhelming for a puppy that isn't prepared for it. If this happens a few times and later, when the puppy is older, an uncomfortable procedure or examination is done, a fear of the vet is put in place which is very difficult to eradicate later on.

To prevent this from happening, your puppy should be well socialized by the breeder so that at the time of his first

ABOVE: *Try to avoid unpleasant encounters with other dogs by keeping your puppy's attention focused on a toy whenever an unfriendly or potentially aggressive dog appears.*

LEFT: Encounters like these can be very frightening for your puppy if he is shy and he is having too many new experiences at once. Ensure that he has many similar encounters that are pleasant soon afterwards or he may always be worried about visiting the vet.

vaccination he is already happy to meet and be handled by strangers. You should take him out and about so that he gets used to meeting other animals and being in new situations. If you develop a good relationship with him, he will view humans as trustworthy and he will also look to you to protect him in times of uncertainty. If, after all this, your puppy is still shy, ask if you can take him back to socialize with the nurses and to practise having him examined when more time is available. A good veterinary practice will welcome this as they know that puppies who have had good experiences early on make much easier, more friendly patients when they become adults.

RIGHT: Watch for signs that your puppy is anxious and take action to make the situation more pleasant for him.

94

TERRITORIAL AGGRESSION

PUPPY FACT

Postmen are more likely to be bitten than other visitors as they do something suspicious (rattling the letter box) and appear to run away when barked at. Dogs become very confident of their ability to deal with them.

Some breeds are more likely to be territorial than others. German Shepherd Dogs, for example, are renowned for their desire to protect their homes and gardens. Territorial aggression, however, is a manifestation of a deep-seated mistrust of people and can be prevented in the same way as nervous, defensive aggression. If you have acquired a puppy with a shy, sensitive, reactive nature, it is particularly important to make a very big effort to socialize him adequately, especially with children who are more at risk when climbing into a garden or yard.

As well as socialization and building a good relationship with your puppy, it is also advisable to get him used to meeting many people at the boundaries, such as at the gate, over the fence and at the front door. Hang a favourite toy by the front door and keep titbits handy to give to visitors as they approach. If visitors represent titbits and games with toys, it is likely that your puppy will have a positive attitude to them throughout his life.

RIGHT: *Territorial aggression is caused by fear of strangers entering the property. If this dog thought of everyone as a friend, he would not have such a strong desire to guard his home.*

95

ADOLESCENCE AND NEUTERING

P uppies reach puberty at about six months of age. At this time, hormonal changes in their bodies are likely to have a very big influence on their behaviour.

BELOW: Most male adolescent dogs will spend a lot of time sniffing and marking their territory. Finding out which other sexually active dogs live in their vicinity becomes very important to them.

MALE DOGS

In males, behaviour designed to lead them to mating will begin in earnest. A male puppy may try to mount bedding, cushions, other dogs, small children and people's legs. This is normal but should be firmly discouraged if it involves people or other animals. He may also be restless and may try to escape to roam the neighbourhood. He is also likely to be more competitive with other male dogs at this time. These behaviours will reach a peak during adolescence and will usually subside gradually as the dog matures. However, if they do not, castration will take away any unwanted behaviour and get rid of any sexual frustration.

FEMALE DOGS

In females, behaviour changes will often occur a few weeks before the onset of the first season. A female puppy may appear distracted, bad tempered and, generally, unlike her usual self at this time. There may be a temporary breakdown in being clean in the house and she may be unwilling to respond during training sessions. This behaviour may continue for a few months until the season is over and her hormone

levels return to a resting state. Having her spayed after the season will prevent a repetition of any difficulties when the next season occurs and will prevent unwanted litters.

FERAL DOGS

In feral dogs, there is a natural dispersion of puppies at the time of puberty. Adolescent puppies begin to spend longer periods of time away from their mothers and their den and travel further away. In our pet dogs, you may notice a gradual distancing as your puppy matures. He may become less dependent on you and less inclined to do as you say. His interest in the world around him takes precedence over his interest in you and this can be very disconcerting. Try not to lose heart at this time. There is likely to be a period of difficulty until your puppy becomes an adult at twelve to eighteen months; this is also the time when adolescent chewing will occur (see page 32). Continue training and playing with your puppy and, gradually, he will come back to you. Don't give up – things will get better!

ABOVE: *Adolescence is a time when puppies begin to take less notice of you and more notice of the world around them. Disheartening as this is, it is only a short time before they begin to mature into adults.*

97

ENERGETIC PUPPIES

6

All puppies will be very lively when they are young, particularly during adolescence and early adulthood. However, dogs of certain breeds and from working strains will remain energetic all their lives and are therefore best suited to owners who have an active lifestyle that allows them to exercise together.

Energetic dogs need a combination of physical and mental exercise. Unless you intend to be active with your dog all day, you will need to tire his mind as well as his body. You can do this by playing with him, training him

BELOW: *All puppies need to use up excess energy. Playing with toys is an ideal way to do this.*

ABOVE: *Under-exercised dogs may be boisterous and difficult to control. Providing enough exercise will result in a more relaxed, contented puppy.*

and teaching him games and tricks (see page 117). Providing the right amount of exercise for your dog, both physical and mental, will result in a contented dog that is easier to live with and is less likely to develop bad habits and behaviour problems.

It is important to remember that a dog with lots of energy that was bred to work will be like this every day, even on days when you are feeling tired or ill. Such a dog will be able to cope with the odd day or short spell with limited exercise but will not be able to tolerate prolonged periods with little to do. The consequences of not providing enough exercise for an energetic dog can be exasperating for owners. An under-exercised dog will be constantly active and looking for something to do. It is likely to be boisterous and difficult to control. It may run off on a walk and refuse to obey commands until it has used up some of its excess energy. It may chase things it shouldn't and may bark or be destructive when left alone. To ensure that none of these unwanted behaviours occur, ensure that your puppy gets enough exercise and continues to do so throughout his life.

DO NOT OVER-EXERCISE

Young puppies have soft bones and joints and care should be taken not to over-exercise them or walk them too far. This is particularly true in the case of the large, heavy breeds, such as Irish Wolfhounds. If in doubt, consult your veterinary surgeon for advice.

DOGS FOR ENERGETIC OWNERS

There are plenty of breeds of dogs that are known for being lively and would suit energetic owners. Most of these are direct descendants of working stock. Springer Spaniels, most collies and herding dogs, Jack Russell Terriers and many hounds are likely to have high energy levels. If you want a dog that is playful or will work for you, it is best to own one of the herding or Gundog breeds since they tend to enjoy playing with objects and like to hold them in their mouths.

LEFT: *Springer Spaniels and other breeds that were developed for active work will be energetic and lively throughout their lives.*

Dogs of medium size that have a body shape designed to run, such as the herding breeds, are more likely to be able to keep up with you if you are a jogger or want to take them with you when you ride a horse or bike. A smooth, fine coat will also help if you are intent on fast exercise as they will lose heat faster than a heavy-coated breed that may need to stop often to cool down.

LEFT: *Dogs whose parents were bred to work are likely to be more energetic than those bred as pets or for showing.*

101

IMPORTANT NEEDS FOR A WELL-BEHAVED DOG

Dogs have certain needs that must be met if they are to be contented and well-behaved. If these needs are not met by their owners, dogs may show unwanted behaviour as they try to fulfil them themselves.

THE NEED TO STAY SAFE

This is the most important need since, in the wild, if an animal is not safe it is likely that it will be either injured or killed. If a dog feels unsafe, it may show avoidance behaviour, anxiety, or defensive or territorial behaviour. Once it feels safe, it will begin to attend to its other needs.

BELOW: Puppies that feel safe and supported by their owners will be more relaxed and will show less defensive behaviour than those who are at odds with their family.

If a puppy is well socialized and lives with a sensible, kind owner, it is unlikely that it will need to attend to this need very often.

THE NEED TO MAINTAIN THEIR BODIES

Dogs need to keep fit and to acquire food in order to maintain their bodies in good condition. We provide our pets with enough food for their daily needs, but this does not mean that they lose the desire to exercise. If they had to hunt for their food they would need to run, jump, chase, capture, chew and, then eventually, dig to bury the excess. Dogs that live in our houses still need to do this and, therefore, it is essential that most of their hunting behaviour is diverted into play with toys and other activities that are acceptable to us.

Dogs will also lick their coats and skin in order to keep them free of parasites, foreign bodies and knotted fur. Humans now do this for them and dogs do not seem to miss performing these behaviours once their coats are clean and untangled.

ABOVE: *Digging to bury bones and other objects is a natural behaviour that their ancestors once used to store excess food.*

THE NEED TO REPRODUCE

In our pet dogs, reproduction is no longer a requirement and so we sometimes have our pets neutered. This removes the desire to exhibit behaviour designed to find a mate, such as escaping, roaming, competing with other dogs of the same sex, marking a territory and mounting.

THE NEED FOR SOCIAL CONTACT

In order to be safe, eat and reproduce, dogs need to be part of a social group. If a dog feels isolated, it is likely to exhibit behaviour that changes this, such as attention-seeking behaviour, escaping to find social contact elsewhere, and howling to reunite it with its owners when separated.

PUPPY FACT

Puppies that have all their needs met are content and are more likely to be well behaved than those that are trying to find fulfilment.

PLAYING WITH YOUR PUPPY

Your young puppy will not know how to play games with toys and you will need to teach him slowly. Most puppies like to hold and carry things in their mouths. Some will instinctively chase after an object. All puppies have learnt to play with their siblings by grabbing them with their mouths and by wrestling. You will need to teach your puppy that he cannot do this to you (see page 35) but that, instead, he can have fun with you by playing with toys.

Begin with soft toys if your puppy finds it easier to hold them in his mouth than the harder sort. Keep them moving so that they become more interesting and roll them away from your puppy to entice him to run after them. Praise him when he reaches the toy and encourage him to pick it up. Once he is holding it, do not take it away from him straight away, but wait a while, praising him for doing so. In this way, your puppy will begin to learn that it is rewarding to play with toys and, gradually, you can develop this into a variety of games to play.

USING UP ENERGY

ABOVE: *Use soft toys at first to encourage a reluctant puppy to play, moving on to harder toys as he becomes stronger and more skillful.*

Playing with toys enables owners to use up their puppy's energy without becoming exhausted themselves! Not only can you exhaust your puppy's physical energy by teaching him to retrieve a toy, but you can also use up his mental energy by devising games in which he has to work out how to get the toy back (see page 117). Games with toys are an

LEARNING TO FIND

A young puppy will have no idea of where the toy has gone if you throw it up in the air. It will take him time to learn this move and to begin to look around himself to discover the toy's whereabouts. At first, he will simply gaze into space looking confused.

ideal substitute for all the skills and behaviour puppies would use if they were hunting and, consequently, use up their energy in a way that no other activity can. For the herding breeds that are so interested in chasing moving objects, it is essential that they find a suitable outlet for this behaviour. Failure to do so can result in a dog that becomes obsessed by chasing unsuitable objects, such as bikes, cars, joggers or livestock.

BELOW: *Playing with toys is an excellent way to improve your relationship and use up excess energy.*

PUPPY FACT

Young animals play with others to acquire skills, develop their muscles and learn about their relationship with others.

PLAY WITH OTHER DOGS

Although it is very important to let your puppy play and socialize with other dogs and puppies, it is more important that he learns how to play with people if he is to become a successful pet dog. For this reason, it is important to limit the amount of play he has with other dogs, particularly if you have a dog at home. You should aim to ensure that he spends up to three times as much time playing with humans as he does with other dogs. This will make an allowance for the fact that it will be relatively less exciting for him initially to play human games rather than rough-and-tumble games with other dogs which are so instinctive.

ABOVE: *Make sure your new puppy spends more time playing with you than with your other dog if you have one.*

HOUNDS: A SPECIAL CASE

Most hounds are not very good at playing with objects. They will wrestle with each other, but do not seem to like picking up items and playing with them in the same way as most of the other working breeds. Instead, they prefer running and chasing real animals. This makes them unsuitable pets for owners who are playful and would enjoy playing with their dog with toys.

BELOW: *Hounds are often disinterested in playing with toys and prefer, instead, to chase animals or people if they can.*

NO ROUGH AND TUMBLE

It is not a good idea to encourage a young puppy to play rough-and-tumble games with humans unless you are an experienced dog owner, particularly if your puppy will grow into a large dog. These games usually encourage a dog to bite human hands and arms and to use their strength

LEFT: *Rough and tumble games with littermates are essential for learning how to play with other dogs, but they should be discouraged once your puppy comes to live with humans.*

against you. Dogs that have learned how to bite humans will be much more practised if they need to do so in defence later and so these games are best avoided. It is particularly important that children do not play in this way since a puppy will usually learn that he is stronger, faster and better at being in control as he grows up. Instead, it is better that children learn to play games with toys with their puppy so that they can stay in control.

BELOW: *Play can be used to teach valuable lessons, such as how to be patient.*

GAMES TEACH PUPPIES VALUABLE LESSONS

Puppies learn a lot through play, just as children do. In particular, they learn about communication with humans, about our strengths and weaknesses, and what is acceptable and what is not. Puppies get to know us through play, and we get to know more about our puppy's character. Since puppies are learning all the time, it is important to think about what they are learning while they are playing. Are they learning that it is acceptable to jump up and put paws on people when they can't quite reach the toy? Are they learning that it is acceptable to bite fingers to make hands let go? Are you learning to run after everything that moves fast? By being aware of what our puppies are learning, it is possible to ensure that they learn good things rather than bad ones.

GOOD MANNERS DURING GAMES

Make sure that everything your puppy does when playing will be acceptable if he should do it when he is a fully grown adult. Jumping up to get the toy is a particularly bad habit which can result in broken bones in the elderly or squashed children if it is not discouraged early on. Once your puppy has let go of the toy, ask him to sit and insist he does so before it is thrown again.

Games with toys present a perfect opportunity to teach your puppy to be careful with his teeth. Every time he bites you, even if it is an accident, take the toy away from him and end the game. If this happens every time, he will soon learn to be more careful and will try to keep his teeth away from your skin in future.

LETTING GO OF A TOY

Some puppies can be very reluctant to let go of a toy once they have it in their mouths. Practise taking the toy away when your puppy is very small and it will be easier later on when he is bigger and stronger.

Let him hold the toy for a short time while you praise him and tell him how clever he is. Slowly take hold of the toy from underneath where he cannot see your hand coming. Pull the toy towards you, holding it tightly and keeping it as still as possible. Ask him to 'leave' and, at the same time, produce a small, tasty titbit and wave it under his nose. Be patient and he should let go of the toy to get the titbit. Feed the titbit and throw the toy again for him to chase. In this way, you will soon be able to get him to leave the toy on command. Once he lets go every time you ask, offer the titbits at random as a reward.

ABOVE: *Teaching your puppy to leave a toy on command is a useful exercise. Begin by offering incentives so that it is worth his while to give up his favourite game.*

PLAY ON A WALK

Always take toys with you when you go for a walk. Playing games with your puppy every now and then will keep him interested in you and help encourage him to listen to you. Walks should be a time for education as well as exercise and it is good to get into the habit of doing very small training sessions throughout the walk.

A FAVOURITE GAME

With humans, dogs tend to play one of three games. These are chase games, tug-of-war games and games with squeaky toys. Your puppy will have a preference for one type of game. This will be determined mostly by his genetic make-up. For example, collies and other herding dogs prefer chase, Bull Terriers prefer tug-of-war, and Jack Russell Terriers prefer games with squeaky toys. If your dog has a favourite game, play this game with him. Trying to change the game to one you prefer does not always work and can result in a frustrated puppy that prefers not to play with you at all.

CONTROLLING THE CHASE

If your puppy enjoys chase games and is very excited by movement, it is important that you keep control

OPPOSITE: *Taking toys and treats with you enables you to do short training sessions on a walk so that your puppy learns to respond to commands in all situations.*

BELOW: *Bull Terriers love to play tug-of-war and this puppy is no exception. If you have a strong-willed puppy, ensure you win more games than you lose.*

111

of these desires. If you begin while your puppy is still young, it will be easier to control him when he attempts an inappropriate chase later on.

A good way to teach him to control his desire to chase is to make him wait while a toy is thrown. Only teach this once he is very keen to chase the toy. Before you throw the toy, ask him to wait and slip a piece of line through his collar. Hold both ends and throw the toy. Make him wait until he calms down and then ask him to 'fetch' and let go of one of the ends of the line so that it slips through his collar. By doing this he will learn to deal with the frustration of not being able to chase whatever he wants and will learn to listen to you rather than to his own desires.

KEEP IT FUN

Games should be fun for both you and your puppy. Keep sessions short and stop before either of you gets too tired. The more exciting you make the games, the more your puppy will enjoy playing with you. Children are so successful at playing

BELOW: *Games should be fun for both you and your puppy. If you are getting bored, stop, try a new toy or think of a different game to play.*

games with puppies because they are active, squeaky, enthusiastic, competitive, and do not feel inhibited so try to be as child-like as possible.

TEACHING YOUR PUPPY TO RETRIEVE

Teaching your puppy to retrieve is a useful exercise as it enables you to get the toys back again easily during games. It is also the basis of most other games and many tricks that you can teach your puppy. Getting a good basic retrieve helps to put you in control of the games and helps to build the right sort of attitude between you and your puppy.

ABOVE: *Puppies like to compete with you to see who can keep the toy for the longest time. Chasing your puppy when he has the toy will teach him to stay out of reach, and it will be very difficult to teach him to retrieve later.*

113

It is best to begin while your puppy is still very young and has not yet learned to avoid you when he has something in his mouth.

1 Tease him with a soft, lightweight toy that he can easily carry.

2 When he is really interested in it, throw it a small distance away and encourage him to run forward and pick it up. If he runs forwards, but does not pick it up, flick it away from him so that the movement entices him to grab and hold it. When he is holding the toy, praise him and encourage him to come to you. If necessary, run backwards to encourage him to follow.

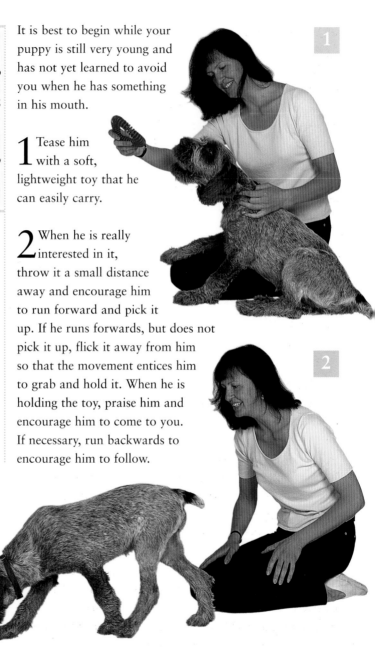

114

3 As he comes up to you, keep your hands away from his head and neck as this may cause him to avoid you in an effort to keep his toy. Praise him enthusiastically and stroke his body to encourage him to stay with you. After a few moments, take the toy away. As soon as you have it, throw it for him to chase again so that he learns that giving the toy to you is a good idea as it results in another game.

3

If he has already learnt to avoid you when he has a toy, attach a lightweight line to his collar and use this to manoeuvre him back to you. Spend more time reassuring him that you will not take the toy as soon as he reaches you, and, gradually, he will learn that it is safe to take the toy to you when he has it.

Remember to keep sessions short and to make them fun. Try not to get cross if your puppy does not get everything right all the time. The retrieve is a complicated exercise that relies on a number of elements. The puppy has to chase the toy, pick it up, carry it and come back to you. This takes both considerable co-ordination and complex thought processes. If your puppy does not make all the connections straight away, try not to lose heart, but keep practising. Eventually, all the elements will come together and you should have a perfect retrieve.

More control

Once you have a very enthusiastic retrieve, begin to put in some control – not too much or you will spoil the fun and reduce your puppy's enthusiasm to play. Begin by asking your puppy to sit before you take the toy. He may spit out the toy as he sits since his mind will have moved on to performing this action for you rather than holding on to the toy. If this happens, encourage him to pick up the toy again and then ask him to sit again. Once he becomes more familiar with this exercise, he will be able to hold on to the toy at the same time. Eventually, you should be able to progress to the stage of asking him to sit in front of you and let go of the toy when you ask. This will make games with him very easy to play.

BELOW: *Encourage your puppy to hold objects in his mouth by praising him whenever he picks something up and carries it.*

Carrying difficult items

As your puppy becomes more experienced at chasing and retrieving his toys, begin to substitute other items for him to fetch and bring back. Begin with items that are easy to hold and soft to bite onto, and then progress to objects that are harder and that dangle down from his mouth. Fetching a bunch of keys, for example, will be very difficult because they are made of hard metal and fall about loosely when carried. If you want your puppy to be happy to carry anything for you, work up to such items slowly.

GAMES AND TRICKS

Once you have taught your puppy the basic obedience exercises (see Chapter 4) and how to retrieve (see page 113) you can move on to teaching a variety of different games that will be fun for both of you.

GAMES

When you are teaching a new game, practise in short sessions, break down the game into small sections, and always end the session on a successful note so that your puppy is enthusiastic next time.

FIND A TOY

This game involves your puppy learning to find an object hidden somewhere in the house or garden. Once your

BELOW: *Teaching your puppy to find toys hidden somewhere in the house uses up lots of his energy without tiring you.*

PUPPY FACT

Break down tricks into small sections. Teach the last section first so that you will be working towards what your puppy already knows when you begin to teach the section before it.

puppy knows the game it can provide him with hours of fun and activity while you sit down and rest!

Begin by showing your puppy his favourite toy. Hold his collar and throw the toy so that it lands out of sight. Release him and ask him to 'find'. Practise this over several sessions and then, at the beginning of the next, have the toy already planted in position and send him to 'find' it. Always praise and make a big fuss of him when he finds it. Gradually progress to hiding the toy in more difficult places further away until he will search the whole house or garden with little encouragement. Eventually you can hide different objects as well, some of which may contain food for added interest.

PLAYING MESSENGER

This is fun for families, especially those with children. Begin by asking your puppy to 'go to ...' a named person who is sitting opposite you in the room. The named person offers a treat and lures the puppy to them. Repeat several times over several sessions until he will run to the named person when you give the signal.

RIGHT: *This puppy is being taught to play messenger. This is an enjoyable way for your puppy to interact with everyone in the family.*

118

Ask the person to go out of the room and repeat. Help the puppy out if necessary until he gets the idea and make sure he is well rewarded by the person he finds. Repeat until he can 'go to' all the people who live in the house. You can then teach him to carry objects to them, or tuck messages in his collar to make it fun for humans too.

FETCH AND CARRY

This is easy if you have taught your puppy to retrieve objects other than his toys. (see above). Once he can do this, you can ask him to help you when you do jobs around the house and garden. Begin by throwing easy-to-carry objects (such as a tin of dog food) and asking him to 'fetch'. As he brings it back to you, praise him and walk away a few paces, encouraging him to follow. Praise him well and take the object, giving him a tasty food treat as you do so.

Gradually, you can build up to different objects carried for longer. Eventually, he will be really useful to have around when you have got too many things to carry yourself.

ABOVE: *Teaching your puppy to fetch and carry objects enables him to help you around the house and will make his life more interesting too.*

119

Fetch my slippers

If you would like your puppy to learn to fetch named objects, such as slippers or newspapers, begin by offering him the choice between two toys. Put them out in front of him and ask him to fetch the toy that he is most likely to pick up. If he brings back the wrong toy, take it quietly and ask him again to 'fetch the ...'. As soon as he picks up the right toy, show him how pleased you are. Keep practising, over several sessions, until he will retrieve the named toy from a group of other toys. Then move on to teaching him the names of other objects you want him to bring back in a similar way.

ABOVE: *Teaching your puppy to do things for you such as fetching your slippers makes him useful and gives him a job to do.*

TRICKS

Tricks are easy to teach and should be fun for your puppy and spectators. Do not teach anything that is demeaning or hazardous (do not teach puppies to jump until they are mature as it can injure growing bones and joints). Keep lessons short and fun and always end on success.

Hi five!

Asking a puppy to give a paw or shake hands is an easy trick to teach. With your puppy sitting in front of you, tickle the hairs behind one of his front paws gently until he lifts his foot. As he does so, ask him to give a paw and praise him well. Lift the foot up gently on the flat of your hand at first and feed a treat. Gradually progress until he will offer a paw to be shaken on command. You can also progress this if you want to by withholding the treat until he lifts his paw higher. Gradually you can get him to 'wave' in this way, or do a 'hi five' by putting out your hand to meet his paw as it begins to come down.

Which one?

This trick involves teaching him to use his nose to find out which flower pot the treat is hidden under and to indicate which one it is by placing his paw on top. It is a complicated trick so you will need to break it down into stages. Begin first by teaching him to put his paw on top of a flowerpot to receive a treat. Then get him to decide between two pots, one of which has food underneath. Gradually work up to more pots.

ABOVE: *Giving a paw is one of the easiest tricks to teach.*

Throw it away

Teaching your puppy to put rubbish in the bin is a very useful trick. Begin by putting a few treats in a small cardboard box and letting him run to the box to eat them. When he is enthusiastic about running to the box, stop putting treats in the box, attach a thin line to

RIGHT: *The paw shake can be developed into a 'wave' by asking for a more exaggerated response each time.*

121

his collar and give him a small ball of screwed up paper to carry. Use the line to stop him from reaching the box if he drops the paper. Bring him back a little and ask him to carry the paper again. When he gets to the box, he should put his head inside and drop the paper so he can eat the treats. You need to rush to the box so that you are there to feed him treats as he raises his head. Repeat often until he learns that he needs to take the paper to the box in order to get the treats. Replace the box with a rubbish bin (using a rubbish bin at first may encourage him to look in rubbish bins for food). Gradually, you can move further away from the bin so that, eventually, he learns to run to the bin, put the paper inside, and run back to you for a treat. This is quite a complicated trick so do not worry if it takes you a long time to teach it.

BELOW: *This puppy can take the handkerchief out of his owner's pocket and give it to him whenever he sneezes.*

OTHER TRICKS TO TEACH

Be as inventive as you like when it comes to teaching tricks. You could teach your puppy to shut the door or pull a handkerchief out of your pocket when you pretend to sneeze. Tricks that entertain people will be enjoyed by your pet if he is well socialized as he will thrive on their interest and laughter. Tricks that use your dog's natural abilities will be easiest to teach, i.e. tricks that involve using paws will interest terriers, tricks that involve movement and catching objects will be enjoyed by collies, and tricks involving food will win over most hounds and many of the dogs in the Gundogs group.

DOG SPORTS

Dogs sports are games for adult dogs. Competitions are held nearly every week around the country for the five different sports and many dogs attend.

AGILITY

Dogs run a course of jumps, tunnels, hoops, weaves, high walks and A-frames against the clock. Once they have learned to negotiate the obstacles, most dogs love this sport as it combines speed, agility and excitement.

BELOW: *Agility is a sport that most dogs love to take part in.*

PUPPY FACT

Tricks should be fun for both you and your puppy. Choose something which is amusing, but avoid anything which is demeaning or could be dangerous.

FLYBALL

Dogs run down a course of small jumps, press the pedal of a machine that throws out a ball, catch the ball and run back over the jumps to finish. This sport is performed by teams against the clock and the dogs often scream with excitement until they are released.

WORKING TRIALS

This sport includes all the training exercises that police dogs learn to make them useful at their job. They learn to

track, search for lost items, jump a
2-metre (6-foot) scale, a clear jump,
a 3-metre (9-foot) long jump, walk
to heel, retrieve a dumbbell, come
when called, stay out of sight of
their handler, and be sent away in
any direction the handler indicates.
There are many elements to learn,
but competing with your dog in this
sport gives you a partnership with
him that most people never achieve.

OBEDIENCE

Dogs learn to walk closely to heel,
come when called, retrieve a
dumbbell, be sent away as directed,
stay, and retrieve a scented cloth
from others with no scent.

DANCING WITH DOGS

This is a new sport but one that
is already very popular. The dog
learns to do certain movements in
response to signals from the handler.
Once choreographed with music
the resulting 'dance' can be a very
impressive display to watch.

RIGHT: *This dog has learnt to scale
a 2-metre (6-foot) jump from a
standstill during training for a
working trials competition.*

USEFUL ADDRESSES

Association of Pet Behaviour Counsellors
PO Box 46, Worcester WR8 9YS Tel: 01386 751151
email: apbc@petbcent.demon.co.uk website: www.apbc.org.uk

Association of Pet Dog Trainers
Peacocks Farm, Northchapel, Petworth,
West Sussex GU28 9JB

The Blue Cross
Shilton Road, Burford, Oxon OX18 4PF
Tel: 01993 822651

The Kennel Club
1-5 Clarges Street, London W1Y 8AB
Tel: 0171 493 6651

ACKNOWLEDGEMENTS

The publishers would like to thank Jenny and Tony Orchard of Five Acres Boarding Kennels, Cattery and Dog Training Centre, Banbury, Oxon, for their kind assistance in organising the photography, and their dogs, Loki the German Shepherd, Quilly the Golden Retriever, Beattie and Thistle the Labrador Retrievers and Poppy the Cavalier King Charles Spaniel. Our thanks also to the following individuals and their dogs for appearing in the special photographs in this book:

Jenny Aldous and her Golden Retriever, Penny
Lisa Barnes and her Springer Spaniel, Daisy
Mrs Beecham and her Labrador, Hector
Mr and Mrs Brown and Bonny
Sally Brownson and her Dobermanns, Bella, Trudy and Charlie
Annie Cooling and her Border Terrier, Peggy
Angela Cross and her deerhound, Phoebe
Mrs Devlin, Liam and Benji
Roland Dodd and his Boxer puppies
Ann Fairweather and her Bichon Frise, Calli
Pam Horne and her English Pointer, Archie
June Hutt and her Cavalier King Charles Spaniel, Jupiter
Michele Leach and her Spinone, Poppins
Jenny Long and her Standard Poodle, Polo
Freda Masterson and her Border Collie, Tess
Mrs Neville, Jessica and Zack and their Chow Chow, Sinba
Elizabeth Newman and her Airedale Terrier, Claude
Julia Pick and her Staffordshire Bull Terrier, Oz
Eve Scarlett and her whippet, Danny
Tim Scott Andrews and his lurcher, Cyd
Zoe Summerell and her Springer Spaniel, Mollie
Dave and Mandy Timms and their Border Collie, Glen
Joanna, Zena and David Ugolini and their Cocker Spaniel, Jasper
Hazell Williamson and her German Shepherd Dog, Topsy

INDEX